MIDLOTHIAN PUBLIC LIBRARY

STRANGE BUT TRUE

STRANGE BUT TRUE

Chicago

TALES OF THE WINDY CITY

Thomas J. O'Gorman and
Lisa Montanarelli

INSIDERS' GUIDE®

GUILFORD, CONNECTICUT
AN IMPRINT OF THE GLOBE PEQUOT PRESS

Produced in 2005 by
PRC Publishing
The Chrysalis Building
Bramley Road, London W10 6SP, UK

An imprint of **Chrysalis** Books Group plc

© 2005 PRC Publishing

INSIDERS' GUIDE® is a trademark of The Globe Pequot Press.

Cover and text design: Sean Walsh and Matt Windsor
Photo credits: front cover © Chrysalis Image Library

Library of Congress Cataloging-in-Publication Data available on request.

ISBN 0-7627-3680-1

Printed in Malaysia
First Edition/First Printing

977.311

STRANGE BUT TRUE
Chicago

Introduction 6

Part I: Strange But True .14

Part II: Law & Disorder 72

Part III: Urban Myths 130

Part IV: Oddballs & Weirdos 170

Part V: Only in Chicago 212

Sources 256

Introduction

In 2004, Chicago became the first municipality to put itself up for auction on eBay. The Windy City has always been a wheeler-dealer and an overachiever, pushing the limits of the possible. Who can forget Carl Sandburg's description of that fiercely industrious, multitasking and perhaps slightly schizophrenic bully: "Hog Butcher for the World, Tool Maker, Stacker of Wheat, Player with Railroads and the Nation's Freight Handler; Stormy, husky, brawling, City of the Big Shoulders?" A.J. Liebling called Chicago "the Second City." Now it's the third largest after New York and L.A. But Chicago won't settle for anything less than first—like a little brother who overcompensates by powerlifting and cheating in student government elections.

Chicago's strange recorded history began in the 1670s, as the French explored and colonized the Great Lakes region. The word "chicagou"—which first appeared on a French map in 1684—means "striped skunk" or "wild leek" in the language of the Illinois Indians. In 1785, a Haitian-born black man named Jean-Baptiste Point de Sable (also spelled DuSable) built a farm on the present site of the Tribune Tower. Since the 1920s, black Chicagoans have been fighting to get the city to recognize de Sable's role in its history. There's a DuSable Museum and a park in the works. Fans are also pushing for a lifelike sculpture, though no one knows what de Sable looked like. One forensic scientist hopes to dig up his bones and reconstruct his facial features based on his skull.

In the 1795 Treaty of Greenville, the U.S. wrested large portions of the Midwest from a group of Native American tribes. According to one story, Chicago was not originally part of the treaty, but General "Mad Anthony" Wayne demanded that the Indians surrender the "French Fort" pictured on the badly drawn maps of the time. The tribes had no idea what he was talking about. There had never been a fort in that area. But Mad Anthony insisted, until the Indians said, "Fine. Take the fort. It's yours." So the US got Chicago.

Chicago incorporated as a town in 1833 and as a city in 1837. Fires posed a problem from the start. Before fire hydrants and fire hoses, the state-of-the-art technology was a bucket brigade—a line of people who passed buckets of water from hand to hand.

In 1860, the city hosted the very first Republican National Convention, giving local politicians a chance to test their ballot-box-stuffing skills on a national scale. Mayor "Long John" Wentworth issued false credentials, stacked the convention hall with delegates who supported his candidate, and turned other delegates away at the door. He thus ensured that the Republicans nominated a virtually unknown man—Abraham Lincoln.

Lincoln was Illinois' favorite son. After his assassination, Chicago evicted its dead from City Cemetery to make room for Lincoln Park. Work crews were busy digging up the dead and carting them across town when fire broke out. The empty graves saved hundreds of lives, as people took shelter six-feet-under from the Great Fire of 1871.

The blaze lasted two days and razed three-fifths of the business district. Clearly someone had to answer for this. The press blamed Catherine O'Leary, an Irish immigrant who was allegedly milking her cow Daisy, when the bovine kicked over a kerosene lamp and lit the barn on fire. O'Leary and Daisy the cow died in shame. The city council only absolved them in 1997.

The Great Fire didn't curb Chicago's meteoric rise on the prairie. Between 1830 and 1880, the city swelled from a tiny outpost into the nation's second largest urban center. The population passed one million in 1890. Chicago was the fastest growing city on earth, thanks to its flat, open location. At the juncture of the Great Prairie and the Great Lakes, the city had access to the Atlantic Ocean through the Erie Canal and to the Mississippi River through the Illinois and Michigan Canal, which opened in 1848. In 1848, the nation's rail lines also met in Chicago—making it the hub of the Heartland, linking eastern manufacturers to western agriculture. Chicago soaked up a little of each and remained an amalgam, a split personality, which was part bustling metropolis, part cow town.

The Chicago Stockyards opened in 1865, and for almost a century, the Windy City was meatpacking central. Taking advantage of wartime shortages, meat moguls like Philip Danforth Armour introduced refrigerated railcars and shipped pork around the country. Armour's "disassembly line" for butchering hogs inspired Henry Ford's assembly line for the Model T.

Not everyone found the disassembly line inspiring. The nascent labor movement rightly saw that the value of labor was declining with the breakdown of the manufacturing process into small, isolated tasks requiring little skill. The factories and slaughterhouses employed swells of immigrants from Germany, Ireland, Italy, Lithuania, Poland, and other nations. By 1870, Chicago's foreign-born population reached 48 percent—a larger proportion than any other place in North America. Most immigrants worked blue-collar jobs and labored 10 to 12 hour days, six days a week with little pay. The wealth belonged to only a privileged few.

Some say that the Haymarket tragedy had to happen in Chicago, with its rabid industrialism, machine politics, sprawling immigrant populations, and radical labor movement. On May 4, 1886, police tried to break up a peaceful labor rally, when some unknown assailant hurled a bomb into their ranks. The bomb sparked a riot, killing cops and civilians. Afterward, the panicked police rounded up every rumored radical in town. It was the nation's first Red Scare, and the ensuing trial was a farce. The bailiff boasted that he had stacked the jury panels with people biased against the eight working-class defendants, who were anarchists and mostly German immigrants. The judge, who spent much of the trial chatting with pretty women sitting next to him on the bench, sentenced seven men to death, even though no evidence linked any of them directly to the bombing. In 1893, the governor pardoned the defendants, but it was too late for the five of them who had already been put to death.

The Haymarket trial embodied Chicago's strangeness in more than one sense. In the nineteenth century, most Chicagoans came from other cities or countries and this was reflected in the Haymarket trial. Virtually everyone involved—the eight defendants, the police officers, the defense attorneys, prosecutors, jurors, and judge—was born outside the city. Even the mayor, Carter Harrison, didn't move to Chicago until the age of 30.

In 1893, this city of strangers welcomed 27.5 million people—almost half the total population of the US at that time—for the World's Columbian Exposition. City boosters made such a longwinded fuss that *New York Sun* editor Charles Dana supposedly dubbed Chicago the "Windy City"—though the moniker appears in newspapers as early as 1876.

The six-month fair featured such exciting exhibits as the Ferris Wheel and Buffalo Bill Cody's Wild West Show. Buffalo Bill had to perform outside the fairgrounds because his cowboy extravaganza was considered too lowbrow. But his show proved so entrancing that many festival goers never made it to the fair. They thought Bill's Wild West Show was the whole shebang.

Buffalo Bill wasn't the only one snubbed who later had his revenge. Bertha Palmer, the unquestioned grand dame of Chicago society, threw a banquet honoring the Spanish infanta. But the infanta refused to dine with the wife of a lowly innkeeper, Potter Palmer of the Palmer House hotel. Five years later, when Mrs. Palmer was in Rome, the infanta invited Bertha to tea. Mrs. Palmer replied that she "could not socialize with the bilious members of a degenerate monarchy." Touché!

The World's Fair spawned countless innovations, including Pabst beer, diet soda, Cracker Jacks, Shredded Wheat, Juicy Fruit gum, and the South Side Levee, Chicago's vice district, which rose as 27.5 million pleasure-seekers swarmed the city. In the early 1900s, the Palmers fled as the south side bred naughty entertainments and gangsters like Johnny Torrio and Al Capone.

From 1897 to 1938, aldermen Michael "Hinky Dink" Kenna and "Bathhouse" John Coughlin ruled as undisputed Lords of the Levee. Bathhouse, a Turkish bath masseur turned politician, spouted bad poetry at city council meetings. His poems often concerned civic matters: "She Sleeps by the Drainage Canal," "They're Tearing Up Clark Street Again," and "Why Did They Build the Lovely Lake So Close to the Horrible Shore?"

Virtually every politician in town was beholden to Hinky Dink and Bathhouse, who controlled the vote by rounding up tramps each election day. The Lords of the Levee also raked in $50,000 a year by requiring every prostitute, pickpocket, and thief to buy tickets to their "annual underworld orgy." Brothel and saloonkeepers had to purchase them in bulk. Distinguished guests included politicians, businessmen, and leading entrepreneurs, like Ada and Minna Everleigh who ran a fine establishment on South Dearborn Street. The 50-room mansion featured Impressionist paintings, gold-rimmed fishbowls, gold spittoons, and offered "company" to discerning gents for up to $500 a night. The Everleigh sisters sent roots so deep into Chicago politics that when the mayor closed their club, they took the Democratic machine down with them.

"Big Bill" Thompson stepped into the vacuum, serving as mayor through most of Prohibition. Chicago turned into a violent gangland as rival bootleggers gunned each other down. Al Capone funded Big Bill's campaigns, and Thompson provided Capone with police protection. But even during this violent era, the city had a loony side. Like a 20th-century Caligula, Big Bill brought horses into the Chicago City Council chambers and staged a rodeo.

Chicago somehow survived Prohibition and the Great Depression, too. In the 1940s, Mayor Edward Kelly turned the Democratic National Convention into a pro-Roosevelt rally and helped rig the stadium's microphone system so the "voice from the sewer" ensured FDR's nomination for an unprecedented third term.

On December 2, 1942, physicist Enrico Fermi and team split the atom on the University of Chicago squash courts. This latest Chicago innovation wrecked far more devastation than Pabst beer, diet soda, Cracker Jacks, Shredded Wheat, Juicy Fruit gum, and the South Side Levee combined. University of Chicago students claim that no matter how deep the snow gets in winter, a ring of snow-free earth surrounds the site of Fermi's radioactive experiments.

During the 1950s, the nation plunged into the Cold War and the McCarthy era. But throughout this conservative and fearful time, the drag queens on Chicago's south side partied on—carrying on a Chicago ball tradition that perhaps dates back to the nineteenth century and continues to this day.

In 1960, Chicago helped muscle another president into the White House, as Mayor Richard Daley put his political nose to the grindstone gathering votes for JFK. The city hosted another Democratic National Convention in 1968, but this time a violent police crackdown on Vietnam War protests shocked the nation. The result was the Chicago Seven trial, a three-ring circus anticipating today's celebrity courtroom drama. All convictions were later overturned because the judge hadn't allowed enquiry into jurors' cultural biases, and the FBI had bugged the defense attorneys' offices with the judge and prosecution's complicity.

Today Chicago is strange as ever. The city still spawns weird inventions, odd odors, and unorthodox political stunts. A local chef cooks with lasers and inkjet printers. Scientists make cyborgs out of robots and eel brains. Museum goers brave animated dung beetles pushing their poop uphill. And in 2004, Cook County Criminal Court Judge Bertina E. Lampkin sent out letters asking the jurors who sat in her court to vote for her. Citizens were scandalized, but Judge Lampkin hadn't done anything illegal—at least not in Chicago.

PART I:
Strange But True

Chicago is an October sort of city even in spring.

— Nelson Algren

I adore Chicago. It is the pulse of America.

— Sarah Bernhardt

In the nineteenth century, Chicago gained a reputation as a strange and dangerous playground, offering escape from the social hierarchies and Puritan history of New England. Anything seemed possible. Politicians rigged elections. Robber barons made vast fortunes butchering pigs, sheep, and cows. Workers waded through hog blood on the slaughterhouse floor. Gangster pimps like Big Jim Colosimo wore diamond-studded belts and hobnobbed with the Chicago elite.

As the city swelled, it grew dark and Dickensian, resembling a chaotic industrial monster. The stockyards saturated the city with an odor of rotting animals and burnt hair. Garbage piled up in poor neighborhoods. Dogs and horses died and decayed on the streets, speckled with flies. Author Paul Lindau called the city "a gigantic peepshow of utter horror, but extraordinarily to the point." Octave Uzanne called it "that Gordian city, so excessive, so satanic."

Other cities might have found such reports disheartening. Not Chicago. The Windy City swelled with civic pride. In 1893, Chicago hosted the stunning World's Columbian Exposition. Entire villages came from Egypt, Algeria, and other distant places to work at the fair. One exhibit hall was massive enough to contain the Great Pyramid, Winchester Cathedral, the U.S. Capitol, St. Paul's Cathedral, and Madison Square Garden. The 27.5 million fairgoers reveled in bizarre novelties—a map of the US made of pickles, a suspension bridge made of soap, a life-size knight on horseback made of prunes, a moving sidewalk, moving pictures, the automatic dishwasher, the vertical file, and the Ferris Wheel.

Chicago seemed unstoppable. In 1900, the city reversed the current of the Chicago River, making it the only river in the world to flow backward. Developers dug tunnels underneath the Loop. When asked what they were doing, they lied and said they were constructing a telephone system. In fact, they built a 60-mile subterranean labyrinth for freight trains. Their plan was abandoned, and everyone forgot about the tunnels—until 1992, when the tubes flooded with 124 million gallons of Chicago River water. Work crews stuffed mattresses and sandbags into the broken riverbed and finally stemmed the flood. But the city still can't stop tampering with the Chicago River. It dyes the water green every Saint Patrick's Day.

Chicagoans are known for numerous zany inventions—some practical, some terrifying. The Twinkie first appeared in Chicago. So did the fire plug and fire pole. Americus Callahan invented the window envelope in the 1890s. In the 1920s, entrepreneur Donald Duncan successfully marketed the parking meter, movie screen, Eskimo Pie, and Yo-Yo. In 1942, Enrico Fermi split the atom on the University of Chicago's squash courts, leaving a worldwide legacy of fear. But Chicago has one menace under control—spray paint, invented by Chicagoan Edward H. Seymour in 1949. In 1995, the city began rigorously enforcing laws against spray paint sales. Local graffiti-busters rush to the rescue at the tiniest sign of tagging. Some say it's easier to buy a gun in Chicago than a spray-paint can.

The Boy Who Stole Jesus

Each holiday season, the city of Chicago displays a nativity scene at Daley Center Plaza. On December 5, 2004 at roughly 3:30 A.M., Matthew Staib, a 19-year-old student at the Art Institute of Chicago, snatched the baby Jesus out of the manger where he lay surrounded by Mary, Joseph, wise men, and sheep. Witnesses pursued Staib, and soon both he and the baby Jesus were in the arms of the law.

According to reports in the *Chicago Sun-Times*, Staib claimed he wasn't "even that drunk. I was just walking around . . . I wasn't even stealing it. I was just walking around with it. I was probably just going to set it down."

The three-foot, six-pound ceramic figurine had been stolen once before in 1999. A couple of days later, a pseudonymous caller, "Thelonius Monk," phoned 911 to say that the Christ child could be found in a Union Station locker.

After the 1999 theft, Jesus was secured in the manger with cables. But Staib claimed the statue wasn't hard to dislodge. "Tell them to better fasten the wire around the baby Jesus' feet," he suggested. *Sun-Times* reporter Annie Sweeney adds, "When Jesus does return, it likely will be with even more security." Wait a second—this sounds like *Weekly World News*. Are we talking about the Second Coming or a porcelain figurine?

Cyborg in Chicago: Eel Brain Controls Robot

It's a cyborg—an animal-machine hybrid. It consists of a tiny two-wheeled robot attached with electrodes to a disembodied eel brain. And it responds to light. Sandro Mussa-Ivaldi, a physiologist at Northwestern University, places the robot inside a ring of lights 3½ feet in diameter. When the lights are off, the robot remains still. But as soon as one of the lights turns on, the robot races toward it. Another light flashes, and the robot veers toward that one. As the lights flick on and off around the circle, the robot turns and charges, always toward the light like a bull in a bullring.

The eel brain controls the robot's movements. When a light switches on, the robot's electronic eyes send signals to microprocessors, which translate them into impulses that the eel brain can understand. The brain returns signals through different microprocessors, which emit the electric impulses that drive the robot's wheels toward the light. Mussa-Ivaldi explains, "There's an element of uniqueness in what we've done, particularly in the fact we've created a closed loop system, where the lamprey brain and the robot are exchanging information."

Mussa-Ivaldi and his colleagues created the cyborg in 2000 by extracting a brain stem from the six-inch larva of a bloodsucking, eel-like fish called a lamprey. The half-inch-long brain stem floats in a phial of salty oxygenated liquid. The researchers attach electrodes to each side of the brain and run wires to each side of the tiny Swiss robot, called a Khepera. The result is a cyborg, combining living tissue with computer technology.

The cyborg, with its eel brain, isn't super-bright, but seems capable of learning. When researcher Karen Flaming covers one of the robot's eyes, only one side of the brain receives impulses, making the robot spin in circles. But after a while, the brain compensates and sends signals to both sides, straightening out its path.

"The focus of our work is not so much to create a cyborg as to create a tool for investigating the organization of the brain," says Mussa-Ivaldi. But in the long run, scientists hope to create prosthetic devices that a disabled person could control with her brain, much as the eel brain maneuvers the robot. For instance, researchers in Atlanta recently implanted an electrode in a quadriplegic patient's brain. When neurons grew inside the electrode, they attached a transmitter, which enabled the patient to guide the cursor on a computer screen by means of thought.

Pink Elephants

In 1902, Chicago alderman "Bathhouse" John Coughlin began building a zoo on some land he owned in Colorado Springs. He purchased an elephant named Princess Alice—a refugee from the Lincoln Park Zoo who had lost part of her trunk in an accidental run-in with a trapdoor. When Alice caught cold in Colorado during the winter of 1906, Coughlin advised the zookeepers to give her whiskey. They offered her a quart, which reportedly cured her cold, but after that Alice became something of a drunk. In place of peanuts, she begged liquor from zoogoers with flasks and passed out after too much booze.

Backrow Seats

There's a way to watch a Cubs game at Chicago's Wrigley Field without buying a ticket, and it doesn't involve sneaking into a stadium or sitting in front of a TV—though it may involve some rather bizarre rental fees. During the 2004 baseball season, property owners across the street from Wrigley Field raked in over $15 million renting out their roofs to Cubs fans during the games.

Taking the World for All its Worth

In 1999, Mary Corcoran met Chicago attorney Joseph P. Dowd in a bar and told him that the Union Pacific Railroad had offered her a $1.4 million settlement in a case involving the death of her husband. After persuading Corcoran that she needed a better lawyer, Dowd phoned a Chicago firm, which examined Ms. Corcoran's case and concluded that she couldn't expect more than $1.4 million. Though the law firm examined her case without charging her, Dowd is still billing Corcoran for a "finder's fee" of 10 percent ($140,000). In 2004, Dowd went back to court, demanding five years' interest in addition to the $140,000.

Christian Modesty

In the mid-1990s, Albert Johnson sued the Cook County Jail because the presence of women guards monitoring the toilet and shower areas was "humiliating" and offended his sense of "Christian modesty." In November 1996, a federal appeals court rejected Johnson's appeal, though one dissenting opinion claimed that the female guards in the restroom constituted "cruel and unusual punishment."

Radio Call-In Confession

A man recently called in to a Chicago radio station bragging about how he took part in a bank robbery. A bank employee tuned in and called the police, who traced the call to Randy Washington's cell phone. Washington and one other man have been charged with robbery, and the FBI is looking for four other accomplices. Washington denies all allegations and claims that he phoned the radio station to win a prize.

"Vomit Slurpers"

Chicago's Peggy Notebaert Nature Museum lies in the heart of Lincoln Park's rich forested lagoons. In the fall of 2001, museum attendance rose 8.3 percent due to a bizarre science exhibit. The "Vomit Slurpers" display piques kids' interest in science by grossing them out, introducing them to the disgusting sights and smells of the animal world. One display shows how and why cats cough up hairballs.

Children also learn that the Old English word for doctor was "leech," because doctors once believed they could cure diseases by using leeches to suck the patients' blood.

I can push a ball of poop 50 times my weight uphill.

The exhibit also features a Dung-Ball Rally, in which an animated dung beetle boasts, "I can push a ball of poop 50 times my weight uphill." The ancient Egyptians called the dung beetle a "scarab" and compared the excrement ball it rolled up hills to the sun crossing the sky.

Kids also learn that Texas farmers import dung beetles because one of these critters can bury 1,000 pounds of cow manure per year.

A life-size see-through model of a cow issues thunderous belches. Museum-goers can look inside to see the inner workings of ruminants. A cow produces roughly 220 quarts of saliva per day, while humans secrete only one. The bovine's tail flips up each time it poops.

Visitors also get to participate in a contest, "Slimy, Slimier, Slimiest." In this TV game show, modeled on "The Dating Game," kids get to vote on who's the slimiest: Helga the Hagfish, Slomo the Snail, or Luke the Sea Cucumber. The TV show explains why each creature should win. Kids vote by pushing buttons on the Slime-O-Meter.

An exit sign reads, "So you enjoy those honey-glazed doughnuts. You are actually enjoying food drizzled in bee barf."

"Vomit Slurpers" is on a North American tour, ending at Space Center Houston in June 2007.

Give de Sable His Due

Since the 1920s, black Chicagoans have been demanding recognition for Jean-Baptiste Point de Sable (or DuSable). A black man born in Haiti, de Sable settled on Chicago River's north bank between 1784 and 1788 and established his farm at the present site of the Tribune Tower. He got along well with the Potawatomi or "fire-keepers," the Native American tribe that lived in the region.

There's some debate about de Sable and his role in Chicago's history. Some say he was Chicago's first permanent non-Indian settler. Others say that the French set up missions and trading posts before 1700, but de Sable is certainly the best-known and best-documented settler in early Chicago.

De Sable spoke many languages, but was illiterate. He signed by mark and later learned to trace his initials. A highly skilled farmer, manager, and trader, he amassed a sizable estate. Some historians claim he also served as a secret British Indian agent. He married a Potawatomi Indian named Catherine and had two children, Jean Baptiste, Jr. and Suzanne. The first birth recorded in Chicago was of Suzanne's daughter, Eulalia Marie Pelletier, born on October 8, 1796.

There is some debate about de sable and his role in Chicago's history.

In 1800, Point de Sable sold his flourishing farm to Jean Baptiste La Lime for 6,000 French livres and moved to Spanish territory. He probably sold his farm because he was loyal to the British crown, and the U.S. government was planning to build a fort in his neighborhood. Resettling in St. Charles (now Missouri), de Sable purchased a smaller farm. But by 1809, his real estate investments failed, and he died in poverty.

In recent decades, Chicago has started to recognize de Sable's role in the city's history. There's the Chicago DuSable League, Friends of DuSable, and the DuSable Museum of African American History. Fifteen years ago, Mayor Harold Washington designated grounds for DuSable Park. In 1987, the U.S. Post Office issued a commemorative stamp. The artist sketched his portrait from imagination, because there is no surviving likeness of the man. This is certainly true of other historical figures.

But some people are intent on erecting a sculpture that actually looks like de Sable. In 2002, forensic scientist Jihad Muhammad and the African Scientific Research Institute tried to exhume de Sable's bones at his gravesite in St. Charles, Missouri. They plan to reconstruct his facial features based on his skull and learn more about his cultural history and genealogy through DNA testing. It's not easy to reconstruct a face from a 200-year-old skull. To avoid damaging the fragile bones, scientists first build a digital model by taking CAT scans. Based on this digital model, a computerized laser beam constructs a physical copy of the skull one layer at a time by tracing cross-sections of the skull on slices of liquid plastic. The process is called "stereolithography." But Mohammed and his research team have not yet found de Sable's remains.

Rest in Peace at the American Fastener Salvage Yard

Andreas von Zirngibl, born in Russia on March 30, 1797, fought Napoleon at Waterloo in 1816. He later moved to Chicago, where he died on August 21, 1855. His last will and testament decreed that he be buried on his own farm and that his grave remain sacred. His tombstone still stands amid the rubble of the American Fastener Salvage yard, north and east of East 93rd Street and South Ewing Avenue.

Infectious Diseases Ravage the City

In 1854, a cholera epidemic killed 5.5 percent of Chicago's population. From 1860 through 1900, the death rate from typhoid fever averaged 65 per 100,000 per year. In 1891, the typhoid death rate reached 174 per 100,000 due to human waste polluting the city's water supply.

Bucket Brigade

Chicago enacted one of its first ordinances in 1835, two years after it was incorporated as a town and two years before it became a city. The "Fire Bucket" law, passed after a rash of fires, required every store in the town to place "one good painted leather bucket" beside each fireplace. At that time, this was state-of-the-art equipment. Before the advent of fire hydrants and fire hoses, people would form a "bucket brigade" and pass buckets of water from hand to hand to extinguish the blaze.

Home Run

On October 1, 1932, the Yankees played the Chicago Cubs at Chicago's Wrigley Field. As Babe Ruth came up to bat, zealous Cubs fans taunted the Yankee Slugger. The "Bambino" stepped up to the plate and gestured with his hand toward center field. On the next pitch, he sent the ball in the exact direction he'd been pointing—and far beyond what Chicagoans call the "Friendly Confines." Ruth's "called shot," as that stunning home run came to be known, was his consummate vengeance against the peanut gallery in Wrigley Field.

State of Alert

Chicago's last opportunity to celebrate a World Series in Major League Baseball came in 1959, when the Chicago White Sox beat the Cleveland Indians in the American League pennant race. Mayor Richard J. Daley, a lifelong White Sox fan who lived two blocks west of Comiskey Park, ordered a salute to the team. Minutes after they won the pennant, the city's air raid sirens wailed. Since it was 1959, the height of the Cold War, people dove into their bomb shelters and ducked under desks and tables to wait for the mushroom cloud—until they

learned that Fire Commissioner Bob
Quinn, also a Sox fan, had set off the
sirens in honor of the pennant victory.
Daley told the press that Quinn was
simply following the orders of the
Chicago City Council, who had passed a
resolution stating "there shall be
whistles and sirens blowing and there
shall be great happiness when the White
Sox win the pennant." The Sox played
the Los Angeles Dodgers in the World

> *Since it was the height of the Cold War, people dove into their bomb shelters and ducked under desks and tables to wait for the mushroom cloud.*

Series that year and lost in six games. No Chicago team has made it to the
World Series since.

Big Brother

The Chicago Park District is taking on-the-job surveillance to a high level—
12,000 miles high. Park Superintendent Timothy Mitchell is working out the
details of a global positioning system that permits Park District supervisors to
locate their work crews from a satellite orbiting the earth. Workers will carry a
device that acts as both a two-way radio and a GPS. The new technology will

increase efficiency and prevent workers from getting lost. But some see it as an invasion of privacy. How long will it be before we're all watched by satellite?

Strangers to the Grave

When his wife of 47 years, Virgie, died in 2002, Robert Thompson bought two adjoining graves in the suburban Chicago Oak Ridge-Glen Oak Cemetery so that he could someday rest beside his wife. He is now suing the cemetery after discovering that someone other than his wife was interred in her plot. Even though he placed a double headstone on the graves, it did not prevent cemetery personnel from the blunder of misplacing his wife in another grave and burying a stranger in hers.

Wedding Chains

Judge Paul Biebel, Jr. is no stranger to weddings. No other judge can top his record for tying the knot among those awaiting trial in Chicago's Cook County Criminal Courthouse at 26th and California Avenue. Each year, Biebel presides over some 50 such marriages inside his judicial chambers. Grooms are usually dressed in orange jail issue jumpsuits. Recently, seven brides said, "I do," in a large group ceremony. What was his strangest set of circumstance? Probably the time two women showed up to marry the same man.

Reversing the Chicago River

In 1887, the city began making plans to reverse the flow of the Chicago River in order to improve the city's sewage system and reduce infectious disease caused by poor sewage. In order to reverse the river's flow, the city built the 28-mile Sanitary and Ship Canal from the river's south branch to Lockport. Locks at the mouth of the Chicago River and at Lockport control the flow of water in the canal. The completion of the canal in 1900 successfully reversed the current, making the Chicago River the only river in the world that flows backward.

World's Columbian Exposition

In 1893, Chicago hosted the World's Columbian Exposition, an enormous six-month fair celebrating the 400th anniversary of Columbus' voyage to the New World. Though largely forgotten today, in its time, the event was considered as monumental and life-changing an event as the Civil War. But the fair might never have happened if France had not shamelessly humiliated the United States in 1889 by centering

Though largely forgotten today, the event was considered as monumental and life-changing an event as the Civil War.

its world's fair, the Exposition Universelle, around an engineering marvel—a tower of Babel that soared one thousand feet into the sky, dwarfing every other manmade structure and all other nations with the glory of France. America was seized with envy and the need to "out-Eiffel Eiffel."

Chicago was swelling with civic pride, having bounced back from the Great Fire of 1871 and ballooned into the nation's second largest city. City boosters fought hard to host the world's fair, to prove to the world that Chicago was more than a hog-butchering backwater.

> America was seized with envy and the need to "out-Eiffel Eiffel."

The World's Columbian Exposition lasted from May 1 to October 9, 1893. The cost totaled $27,245,566.90, not including the three to four million that state, federal, and foreign governments spent on their exhibit buildings. More than five million went into constructing the Jackson Park lakefront site. The entire fair covered 633 acres and drew 27.5 million pleasure-seekers from around the globe. The populace of the U.S. was only 65 million at that time.

The Ferris Wheel

George Washington Gale Ferris, a bridge-builder from downstate Galesburg, Illinois, invented the Ferris Wheel specifically for the World Columbian

Exposition, as Chicago's answer to the Eiffel Tower. Two Brobdingnagian bicycle wheels—264 feet in height, 250 feet in diameter, and 825 feet in circumference—stood 30 feet apart on a 45-foot axle. The axle was the largest piece of forged steel in the world at that time, and it weighed 142,031 pounds along with its fittings. This was heavier than anything that had ever been lifted before, and it had to be mounted on top of eight towers.

A 20,000-pound chain linked a sprocket on the axle to the sprockets on the two 1,000-horsepower steam engines. The Ferris Wheel held 36 wooden cars the size of small railway coaches, each holding 60 people making a total of 2,160 passengers per ride.

The contraption looked extremely fragile and patently dangerous. A project of comparable scope would be unimaginable today as no one would insure it. But every day, thousands of fairgoers paid 50 cents a piece to climb into the cars and soar for 22 minutes above the city. Rumors spread about suicides, including a tale of a pug that jumped to his death. The Ferris Company denied these allegations. The cars had iron grates and windows to keep people from leaping out. But some passengers discovered their fear of heights a little too late.

> *A project of comparable scope would be unimaginable today as no one would insure it.*

One man named Wherritt panicked and hurled himself against the walls with such force that he shattered glass and bent the iron bars. He shook off everyone who tried to hold him back, until one woman, to everyone's shock, yanked off her skirt and threw it over his head like a net. This subdued Wherritt and thrilled the other passengers, who rarely saw female ankles, let alone bare legs.

The Wheel was the fair's most popular attraction, grossing $726,805.50 during its short lifespan. It was dismantled after the Chicago fair, rebuilt in St. Louis for a 1904 exposition, and scrapped in 1906—but its design has been copied all over the world. Ferris also designed a wheel for Vienna, which you can still ride today.

Buffalo Bill

Colonel William Cody, fresh back from his European tour, applied for a concession at the World's Columbian Exhibition of 1893, but the Committee on Ways and Means set high standards for entertainment, and his silly cowboy and Indian shenanigans didn't measure up. They banned him from the fair. Undeterred, Bill leased 15 acres outside the entrance and made for Chicago with his circus of 10 elk, 18 buffalo, 180 horses, 50 Cossacks and Hussars, 97 Sioux, Cheyenne, Kiowa, and Pawnee Indians, 100 former US Cavalrymen, and Phoebe Ann Moses, also known as Annie Oakley.

Cody parked his entourage next to the fair. On April 3, he opened "Buffalo Bill's Wild West and Congress of Rough Riders of the World." His show had been a smash hit in Europe. In Chicago, he instantly packed his 18,000-seat arena. A display at the entrance gate juxtaposed Columbus, "Pilot of the Ocean, The First Pioneer," with Buffalo Bill, "Pilot of the Prairie, The Last Pioneer." The show took off with a Cowboy Band playing "Star-Spangled Banner," followed by a promenade of American, English, French, German, and Russian soldiers.

Annie Oakley and Bill galloped around on horseback, firing their Winchesters at glass balls their crew tossed in the air. Indians pounced upon a stagecoach until Cody and Co. sprang to the rescue. The show climaxed with the "Battle of Little Big Horn . . . showing with historical accuracy the scene of Custer's Last Charge." While Cody sometimes claimed historical accuracy, he was first and foremost a showman. In London,

> Annie Oakley and Bill galloped around on horseback, firing their Winchesters at glass balls their crew tossed in the air.

Buffalo Bill drove a stagecoach around Windsor Castle, when Indians suddenly appeared on British soil and attacked the coach, as it carried four kings and the Prince of Wales.

Cody's Wild West Show sold out every performance. Over the six-month run, he made more than $1 million—roughly $30 million today. He was so close to one of the main gates that some fairgoers thought his show was the fair itself.

In the popular history *The Devil in the White City,* Erik Larson describes the remarkable meeting of Buffalo Bill and famed suffragist Susan B. Anthony. The 73-year-old Anthony was in the Women's Building, contending that the fair should remain open on Sunday, when a self-righteous clergyman posed what he thought was a rhetorical question—would she rather have her son go to Buffalo Bill's Wild West Show instead of church on Sunday? Anthony said yes, because "he would learn far more." Cody, a staunch supporter of women's rights and a big flirt, was so tickled that he mailed Anthony a thank-you note and offered her a box seat at his show. When he spotted Anthony in the audience at the start of a show, Cody charged toward her box and halted in a billow of dust. Doffing his hat with a great flourish, he bowed deeply. Anthony bowed back, "as enthusiastic as a girl," and shook her handkerchief at him. The audience rose and gave them both a standing ovation.

It is given to some cities, as to some lands, to suggest romance, and to me Chicago did that hourly. It sang, I thought, and in spite of what I deemed my various troubles, I was singing with it.

— Theodore Dreiser

Women's Building

At the World's Columbian Exposition of 1893, Chicago grand dame Bertha Palmer organized the Women's Building, which celebrated women artists, writers, and scientists from Helena, the daughter of Timon of Egypt, to Impressionist painter Mary Cassatt. The 1893 fair marked a watershed in the women's movement. The 1876 Centennial Exhibition in Philadelphia had had a Women's Pavilion, but it was controversial, seen as a mark of segregation and second-class status. Suffragists wanted the right to vote, not an art show. In contrast, the Women's Building at the 1893 event was considered a sign of inclusion. The way men treated women had not changed dramatically, but there was a shift in the leadership of the women's movement. Wives of a Gilded Age industrialists, like Bertha Palmer, who presided over Chicago high society, were replacing the previous generation of strident East Coast patricians such as Susan B. Anthony, Elizabeth Cady Stanton, and Julia Ward Howe.

Suffragists wanted the right to vote, not an art show.

As chair of the Board of Lady Managers, Mrs. Palmer took charge of anything and everything involving women at the fair. Bertha was an avid collector of

French Impressionist paintings, but she did not know much about architecture. She invited women from around the world to contribute architectural ornaments for the Women's Building. Thousands of sculptures, doors, columns, and window grills poured into Chicago, and Bertha insisted that the architects include all of them in the construction. As Bertha's secretary wrote, "I think it would be better to have the building look like a patchwork quilt, than to refuse these things which the Lady Managers have been to such pains in soliciting." When the young architect, Sophia Hayden, turned down a number of donations, Mrs. Palmer waged such a grisly battle of icy smiles and poisonous politeness that Hayden had "a severe breakdown" and was discreetly removed from the fairgrounds and confined to a sanitarium.

> Thousands of sculptures, doors, columns, and window grills poured into Chicago.

Infanta Snubs Bertha Palmer

The Infanta Eulalia of Spain, daughter of Queen Isabel II and youngest sister of King Alfonso XII, spent a week at the World's Columbian Exposition. Chicago society saw her stay as a chance to cast off the city's hog-butchering reputation and demonstrate its refinement. City boosters met the 29-year-old princess at her train and escorted her to the Palmer House, one of the nation's premier hotels, where she stayed in the most luxurious suite. Bertha Palmer planned a reception for her at the Palmer mansion and had a throne built on a raised dais, so she could sit above the other guests.

But the infanta noticed that her hostess had the same name as her hotel. As her entourage prepared to leave for the banquet, she asked the US ambassador if Mrs. Palmer was any relation to the innkeeper. When he replied that they were married, the princess proclaimed that she could not possibly accept an invitation from an "innkeeper wife." This sent the assembled diplomats into a tailspin.

Eventually they prevailed upon the royal to make an appearance at the Palmers' home.

Eventually they prevailed upon the royal to make an appearance at the Palmers' home. Bertha welcomed her with warmth and delicacy and denied any awareness of a snub, though the local newspapers skewered the infanta.

Five years later, Mrs. Palmer visited Rome, where Eulalia was living in exile during the Spanish American War. When the banished princess invited Mrs. Palmer for tea, Bertha declined, noting she "did not socialize with the bilious members of a degenerate monarchy." The Chicago press cheered Mrs. Palmer, who had finally "had her day with the infanta."

Inventions and Innovations

The World Columbian Exposition of 1893 introduced a number of inventions and new products:

- The movable sidewalk, now an airport staple

- The Ferris Wheel

- Gray's Teleautograph, a machine that electrically reproduced handwriting at a distance

- Thomas Edison's Kinetograph (This forebear of the movie projector showed the first moving pictures.)

- The first zipper

- The first all-electric-powered kitchen

- The first commemorative stamp set

- The first picture postcards, compliments of the US Postal Service

- Cracker Jacks

- Aunt Jemima's—a box that allegedly contained everything you needed to make pancakes

- The US Mint's first commemorative coins (a quarter, half dollar, and dollar)

- Cream of Wheat

- Shredded Wheat (Fairgoers didn't think the product would succeed. Some dubbed it "shredded doormat.")

- Pabst Beer (After winning the fair's best beer award, the brewer renamed it Pabst Blue Ribbon Beer.)

- Juicy Fruit gum

- Diet carbonated soda

- The first hamburger in the United States.

- The vertical file (Melvil Dewey, creator of the Dewey Decimal System, gave us this office necessity.)

Fairgoers also saw a number of novelties that have faded into history:

- A suspension bridge made of soap

- A train made of silk

- A map of the United States consisting solely of pickles

- A life-size knight on horseback made of prunes

- A Statue of Liberty replica sculpted from a block of salt

A Surprise in Every Box

Perhaps the World Columbian Exposition's most enduring legacy is not the neo-classical architecture it made famous or even the Ferris Wheel, but F. W. Ruckheim's unmistakably American caramel-covered popcorn and peanut snack. According to rumor, Ruckheim's very first customers exclaimed, "That's a cracker Jack," as they tasted his concoction. The rest is history. The product is still made in Chicago, and Cracker Jack lovers still fish in the bottom of their box to find the surprise.

> *Cracker Jack lovers still fish in the bottom of their box to find the surprise.*

Fire at the Fair

The summer following the World's Columbian Exposition of 1893, a mysterious fire swept through the empty buildings at Jackson Park, the main exhibition site. The imitation-stone structures were made from a hemp and plaster compound, which burned quickly and easily. In Jackson Park, only one building remains from the fair—the Museum of Science and Industry, which was once the Palace of Fine Arts. A $5,000,000 bond issued in the late 1920s financed a complete restoration of the structure. The Art Institute of Chicago on Michigan Avenue also played a role in the fair, though it wasn't part of the Jackson Park location. It was the fair's Hall of World Religions, the scene of many ecumenical gatherings.

Oz Native

Few Americans know that Lyman Frank Baum, author of *The Wonderful Wizard of Oz* (1900), invented Dorothy and crew while living in Chicago's Humbolt Park neighborhood. Oz Park, a 13-acre area in the Lincoln Park community, was created in 1967 in honor of the author. There are a number of statues of Oz characters throughout the park, including a sparkling Tin Man. This was created by the noted Chicago artist John Kearney, and was added in 1995 at the corner of Webster and Larrabee. The Cowardly Lion at the corner of Larrabee and Dickens was restored in 2001 after an Oz Park Council fundraising campaign. The latest fundraising drive will result in a Scarecrow statue in the Emerald City Gardens area.

Birth of the Playboy Bunny

While Alfred Kinsey was the scientist behind the sexual revolution, Chicago's Hugh Hefner was its first pop-cultural guru. The aldermen renamed one of the major Loop streets in his honor. In December 1953, Hefner, a direct descendant of *Mayflower* passenger William Bradford, tossed aside his Puritan roots and released *Playboy*, a glossy magazine featuring photos of female flesh and celebrating hedonistic bachelordom. The monthly's circulation passed one million before 1960 and peaked at six million in the early seventies. As lord of this sexual and financial empire, Hefner built a stunning Beaux Arts mansion on

Chicago North State Parkway.

In 1959, Hefner and company laid out plans for a Playboy Club. One night when Hefner and Playboy executive Victor Lownes were batting around ideas for negligee-clad hostesses called "Playmates," Lownes' girlfriend Ilse Taurins suggested dressing the girls like the trademark tuxedoed Playboy Rabbit. Hefner had already considered Playboy Bunnies, but dismissed the idea as "too masculine." Ilse offered to have her mother, a seamstress, stitch a sample rabbit costume.

> Ilse offered to have her mother, a seamstress, stitch a sample rabbit costume.

Several days later, Ilse modeled her mom's bunny costume for Hefner and Co. Hefner was smitten, especially by the tail. After numerous refinements and permutations, the Playboy Bunny suit was born, and the first Playboy Club opened in Chicago on February 29, 1960. Ilse's mother's role was, sadly, almost lost to history, but the Bunny costume remains the only non-service uniform that has been granted a U.S. Patent. The Chicago Historical Society and the Smithsonian both have Bunny suits on display.

In interviews, Hefner has often stated that the Bunny empire would never have been born if it weren't for a last-minute decision. Hefner had intended to call his magazine *Stag Party*. Cartoonist Arv Miller had already designed the stag mascot, complete with antlers, cocktail, and smoking jacket, when *Stag Magazine* accused Hefner of trademark infringement. Hefner renamed his publication, and Miller shortened the stag's snout, clipped his antlers, and gave him long ears and whiskers. The Rabbit Head logo was the brainchild of founding Art Director Arthur (Art) Paul. Millions of Bunny fans applaud the last-minute name change— who could imagine a worldwide chain of nightclubs with hostesses wearing antlers on their heads?

Scheduling Snafu at the Y

In December 2004, the executive director at Chicago's New City YMCA lost his job following a scheduling snafu. Parents bringing their kids to a 7 A.M. swim meet at the Y were startled to find the locker rooms crowded with men in dresses. Months earlier, a YMCA member had booked the facilities for a transgender ball and fashion show. The event began at 11 P.M. Saturday night and lasted until 8 A.M. on Sunday. The ball was just winding to a close when the kids showed up for competitive swimming. Scuffles ensued, as parents demanded what the cross-dressers were doing at their children's swim meet.

Book Burning

After the Great Chicago Fire of 1871, no one responded more generously than the English Parliament and Queen Victoria. The queen was especially grieved by news of the vast number of books that had burned in the city's library. She donated her favorite books, signing each one, and called on British authors, publishers, and booksellers to do the same. Chicago soon received a shipment of some 8,000 titles, a testament to British civility and good will. The list of donors included Matthew Arnold, Robert Browning, Benjamin Disraeli, Alfred Lord Tennyson, John Ruskin, and John Stuart Mill.

But Chicago had never had a public library. The fire had, in fact, destroyed several libraries and countless books,

> Chicago soon received a shipment of some 8,000 titles, a testament to British civility.

but these were all private libraries that charged a membership fee.

Embarrassed by the royal gift, leading citizens petitioned Mayor Joseph Medill to found a free public library. On January 1, 1873, the Chicago Public Library opened its doors in an abandoned water tank on LaSalle and Adams Streets. Now, more than 150 years later, many of the volumes signed by Her Majesty have disappeared. Those remaining are the library's treasure—a reminder of the queen who mourned a library that never was.

First U.S. Blood Bank

In 1937, Dr. Bernard Fantus, director of therapeutics at Chicago's Cook County Hospital, created a laboratory that could preserve and store human blood. It was the first "blood bank" in the U.S. (The very first facility was established in Leningrad Russia in 1932.) Fantus' lab facilitated blood transfusions and thus advanced the practice of surgery. Within a few years, blood banks sprouted up in hospitals and communities across the nation.

Prima Donna

Chicago's Lyric Opera, the city's premier arts venue, celebrated its 50th anniversary in 2004. Its "standing-room only" performances are rivaled only by the Chicago Cubs, and the greatest names in opera, including Luciano Pavarotti, have graced its stage. Pavarotti, who starred in such singular works as Tosca, is also known for canceling performances. In 1989, these cancellations and the ensuing drama led the Lyric's no-nonsense manager, the late Ardis Krainik, to announce that Pavarotti was officially persona non grata in Chicago. The renowned tenor never returned.

Sub Above Water

Since 1954, the U-505 World War II German submarine has been one of the most stirring exhibitions at Chicago Museum of Science and Industry.

In 1944, Chicago native Captain Daniel Gallery and the USS *Guadalcanal* task group 22.3 captured the German submarine off the West African coast. Sailors under Gallery's command boarded the U-boat at sea and acted quickly to stem the near loss of the sub, as the Germans tried to scuttle her. The U-505 was the only German man-of-war that the U.S. Navy apprehended in World War II. It contained a code encryption machine that helped the Allies crack the German code and a map that showed how the German navy had re-chartered the oceans and successfully eluded Allied naval vessels. The Germans never discovered that the Allies had captured the sub and towed it to Bermuda.

After the war, Chicagoans raised $250,000 to tow the boat back across the Atlantic through the St. Lawrence River and the Great Lakes to Chicago, where it became a war memorial and permanent exhibit.

For 50 years, the U-boat endured the extremes of Chicago weather just a few hundred yards from the shoreline of Lake Michigan. In 1997, the Chicago Museum of Science and Industry launched a restoration project to move the U-boat indoors and save it from the effects of weather and pollution. The submarine closed in 2004 and reopened in 2005 in its 35,000-square-foot, climate-controlled enclosure.

First Heart Surgery

The medical establishment assumed that heart surgery would be fatal, until Dr. Daniel Hale Williams, a young African-American physician, performed the first open heart surgery in 1893 by removing a knife from the chest of a patient who had been stabbed at a Chicago bar. Against prevailing medical standards, Williams opened the victim's heart and sutured the knife wound to the pericardium, the fluid sac that surrounds the myocardium. The patient survived the surgery and lived for several years. Williams, who received his M.D. from Northwestern Medical School in 1883, also founded Chicago's Provident Hospital and Medical Center, the nation's oldest free-standing, black-owned hospital, in 1891. In 1913, he was the only black charter member of the American College of Surgeons.

This is a frontier town. And it's got to go through its red-blooded youth. A church and a WCTU [Women's Christian Temperance Union] never growed a big town yet.

– George Wellington "Cap" Streeter

Queen Bertha

In the heyday of old Chicago society everyone knew Bertha Palmer—wife of hotel mogul Potter Palmer and queen of the city's elite. But few knew that after

Potter's death in the early 20th century, she could have been a real queen. King Leopold of Belgium, one of Bertha's more ardent admirers, proposed to her. But she was unmoved by the offer and spent the rest of her life traveling the globe as a Prairie aristocrat. She had all the crowns she needed.

Sally Rand's Fans

Sally Rand, born Harriet Helen Gould Beck, came to Chicago in 1932 in a show called "Sweethearts on Parade." Answering an ad for "exotic acts and dancers," she took a job at the Paramount Club, where she first performed her famous "Fan Dance"—a revealing and concealing dance of the seven veils, only Sally used two pink seven-foot ostrich feather fans that she'd picked up at a second-hand shop.

At Chicago's 1933 "Century of Progress" World's Fair, Sally danced in the "Streets of Paris" concession. She showed up for her event driving along the lakefront in a speedboat. Her Fan Dance of May 30, 1933 propelled her to fame. By almost every account, Sally danced in the buff under her seven-foot fans. In fact, she probably wore a body stocking or white theatrical cream. But in an era when women showed less skin, spectators lined up by the tens of thousands, waiting for her to drop a fan by mistake. She never did.

The Chicago Police carted her off anyway, charging her with "lewd, lascivious" behavior. On July 19, 1933, Superior Judge Joseph B. David dismissed the case, saying, "There is no harm and certainly no injury to public morals when the human body is exposed, some people probably would want to put pants on a horse ... When I go to the fair, I go to see the exhibits and perhaps to enjoy a little beer. As far as I'm concerned, all these charges are just a lot of old stuff to me. Case dismissed for want of equity."

They planned this fair to bring business to Chicago, into the Loop. But you could have fired a cannon down State Street and hit nobody, because everybody was out at the fair.

— Sally Rand

Feast for Beasts

Nancy DeFiesta, 60, a veteran of Chicago's Lincoln Park Zoo, used to believe that there was no such thing as a mean lion. Some were simply more aggressive than others. She is eating her words, after narrowly escaping being eaten herself. On the morning September 9, 2004, she was working in the lion house yard when three lions ganged up on her and mauled her neck, head, and arm. It was a horrible way to begin the day.

The big cats apparently tampered with the safety doors designed to prevent such attacks. DeFiesta radioed coworkers for assistance, as she lay on the exhibit's dry moat. Chicago firefighter Ben Hosek climbed down a 15-foot fire ladder into the lion pit, while other rescue workers wielded fire extinguishers, holding the lions at bay. DeFiesta was in shock and could barely move, as Hosek coaxed her up the ladder, stressing the importance of moving quickly. The longtime zookeeper was rushed to the hospital, where she recovered.

One witness reported seeing the lions leap the chasm that separated them from the public. The Chicago City Council honored Hosek for his bravery, and an investigation into the cause of the incident is underway.

The Lady in the Vat

Adolph Luetgert was one of Chicago's turn-of-the-nineteenth-century "sausage kings." By Chicago standards, he was a robust businessman—prosperous, hardworking, and devoted to his wife, Louise. Then Louise vanished. Luetgert told inquiring friends that his wife was visiting family members out of town. But Louise's friends grew suspicious when she never returned. Police searched for clues to her whereabouts. When no evidence of her turned up in the Luetgert home, they combed the sausage factory and drained a large chemical vat looking for signs of her remains. All they found was a gold wedding ring—the only personal effect not consumed in the tank of chemicals. Adolph was promptly arrested. The entire city shivered at the thought of Louise, of the corrosive chemicals, and of what they may have eaten for dinner the previous night.

Sipping Champagne from a Slipper

When Prince Henry of Prussia, the brother of Kaiser Wilhelm II, arrived in Chicago in 1902, local newspapers trumpeted his 183 pieces of luggage and his royal entourage that filled more than 50 rooms at the famed Auditorium Hotel on Michigan Avenue. One day the prince escaped his royal minders, wandered out of the hotel alone and made his way to the Red Star Inn, one of the finest German restaurants in the U.S. Palace aides searched for the prince and found him enjoying a quiet lunch in the restaurant famous for apple pancakes, hasenpfeffer, and great steins of beer.

During Prince Henry's visit, Chicago's most lavish brothel, the Everleigh Club, threw a banquet in his honor. While one of the girls was dancing, she kicked off her shoe, knocking over a glass of champagne. A man nearby noticed that some champagne had spilled into the shoe. He picked it up and drank from it—sipping champagne from a slipper for perhaps the first time. When the other gentlemen saw what he'd done, they borrowed slippers from the women around them, ordered the waiters to fill the shoes with champagne, and toasted the prince.

Mussolini's Gift

An 18-foot Corinthian column from the first century A.D. stands in Burnham Harbor, near Soldier Field. The column dates from the reign of Roman Emperor Hadrian. "Il Duce" himself, Benito Mussolini, presented it to the city of Chicago in 1934 to commemorate a strange happening the previous year when Chicago celebrated its centennial anniversary with a World's Fair known as "The Century of Progress." On July 24, 1933, 24 Italian seaplanes braved a 46-hour trip from Ottobello, Italy to Chicago. Landing in Lake Michigan, the Italian air-aces arrived in "black shirts," the symbol of Mussolini's Fascist regime. Chicago honored their visit by renaming 7th Street "Balbo Drive" after their commander, General Italo Balbo.

Mussolini's gift shocked the archeological community. It seemed outrageous to send a national treasure like Hadrian's Column out of Italy as a gift to a foreign city. But Chicago gladly accepted the gift, and Italian archeologists didn't dare criticize Il Duce.

The Dead Make Room for the Living

Lincoln Park, a rolling plain of grassland botanicals, stretches along the city's lakefront. The park honors Illinois' favorite son, the slain U.S. president Abraham Lincoln. Before the park was built, in the 1870s, a cluster of graveyards occupied the grounds, including the burial sites of some thousand confederate soldiers who died at the infamous Camp Douglas on Chicago's Southside. To create Lincoln Park, the city had to evict the dead and move them to a new location.

Work crews were in the process of digging up the interments, when the Great Fire of 1871 broke out. As fire rained down from the skies, hundreds of people leapt into the empty graves and saved their lives.

Invasion of the Body Snatchers

Hollywood producer Mike Todd was born Avron Hirsch Goldbogen on Chicago's Westside. He married actress Elizabeth Taylor and was perhaps her favorite husband among many. His untimely death caused her much grief.

Todd died in a plane crash in 1958, two years after producing his best-known film—*Around the World in 80 Days*, based on Jules Verne's 1872 novel. Todd's body was flown back to his hometown for burial in the Waldheim Cemetery. He lay undisturbed until 1977, when grave robbers dug up his body and dragged it out of its casket. Police suspected the thieves were looking for jewelry that was supposedly buried with him in the coffin. The desecration was as ghoulish and bizarre as a scene from a sci-fi thriller.

Tong Turf War

During the early 1930s, in Chicago, all eyes were on the bootleggers and violent perpetrators of gangland crime. It seemed as though there were so many mobsters of Italian and Irish origins living in Chicago at one time that they seemed to have the crime scene sown up, with an exclusive hold on mayhem and murder. They certainly made the headlines. But in truth

The Chinese gangsters received little coverage in the press.

Chinese tongs were engaged in a dramatically violent tong war during the late 1920s and early 1930s. There was only so much ink and federal agents to go around, so the Chinese gangsters received little coverage in the press. They carried out their particular brand of bloodshed within the confines of the city's Chinatown, south of the center city. Along the streets thick with pagoda roofs, the rival bosses of the Chinese underworld squeezed out swift and brutal revenge on their enemies on a small piece of turf. Thanks to the antics of the city's other mobsters, the Chinese got away with murder.

Santa Faces Budget Cuts

Facing a financial gridlock, the Chicago Transit Authority streamlined its budget in 2004. No one was spared, not even Jolly Old Saint Nick. Weeks before

Christmas, the CTA cancelled its traditional "Holiday Train"—the elevated cars with twinkling lights that carry Santa around the city between Thanksgiving and New Years. Now that the budget ax has fallen, Santa will have to go back to reindeer.

Cosmopolitan Chicago

Irish Peer, David Parsons, the Earl of Ross, was visiting Chicago from his family seat of Birr Castle in County Offaly. As a U.N. diplomat, Parsons had spent many years in Africa. Riding in a Chicago taxi, he noticed three slashes on the face of his cab driver and recognized the distinctive face markings Yuroba peoples of Nigeria. The Earl enquired in perfect Yuroba if the driver was from Nigeria. The driver marveled at the Irishman's fluency and his knowledge of Shango, the mystical Nigerian god. As they rode to the lunch, both the driver and the Earl laughed at how they'd met far from their native lands in a Chicago taxi on a Chicago street.

> The Earl enquired in perfect Yuroba if the driver was from Nigeria.

Buried in the Airport

Chicago's O'Hare International Airport lies on land that once belonged to a small farming community of hard-working German Protestants, who settled there when Chicago was just rising on the prarie. In the late 1950s, when the city took over the property to build its jet-age airport, two graveyards came as part of the deal. The cemeteries, St. John's and Rest Haven, still lie within the bounds of the airport, which was constructed around them. Both date from the region's agrarian days. St. John's was established in 1837, the same year that Chicago was incorporated as a city. Sharp-eyed travelers can spot the tombstones near one of the runways.

Archbishop Follows His Arm to the Grave

Samuel Cardinal Stritch (1887–1958) served as Chicago's Roman Catholic Archbishop during the 1940s and 1950s. In 1958, he died in Rome, after a catastrophic illness seized him, as he sailed to Italy aboard the liner SS *Independence*. An arterial occlusion shut off the blood supply to his right arm and necessitated its amputation when he arrived in Rome. The cardinal lived for almost 30 days following the surgery. Chicago doctors flew to Rome to consult on his condition. One of them carried the cardinal's arm back to Chicago where it was buried in the archbishops' mausoleum at Mt. Carmel Cemetery. When the cardinal died, he too was flown back to Chicago and entombed in the crypt with his arm.

Rhodes Scholar

After graduating from the University of Chicago in 2004, Ian Desai charted the mythic voyage of Jason and the Argonauts, then traveled by foot, motorcycle, and boat, following Jason's journey along the south shore of the Black Sea.

Though he didn't woo Ariadne, slay the Minotaur, or claim the Golden Fleece, Ian received a different kind of award—a Rhodes scholarship to study at Oxford University for the next two years. The Rhodes scholarship is named after Cecil Rhodes, not after the Greek island.

The Vanishing Airport

Chicago's lakefront airport, Meigs Field, opened in 1948. It was the ultimate urban airport, stretched along the shore of Lake Michigan. In 1996, as the airport's lease was about to expire, Mayor Richard M. Daley proposed turning the airport into a park. Illinois Republicans, led by Governor Jim Edgar, balked at the idea because they relied on the facility to commute to Springfield, the downstate capitol. Daley agreed to extend the lease in 1997. But when the extension agreement fell apart in March of 2003, the mayor leapt into action. In the wee

> *Meigs Field vanished, erased by political muscle Chicago style.*

hours of the morning, as airport preservationists slept, Daley sent city work crews to the airport and had the runways bulldozed, rendering the facility inoperable. Planes caught unawares had to be towed away. Airport proponents accused the mayor's crews of spray-painting their 24-hour surveillance cameras to hide the airport's destruction. Meigs Field vanished, erased by political muscle Chicago style.

Bertha Palmer's Curious Taste in Art

By 1880, Chicago's Potter Palmer was on his way to making his fourth fortune. He and his wife, Bertha, were the hands-down king and queen of Chicago fancy folk. As if to prove their social importance and deep pockets, Potter demonstrated his love for Bertha with an opulent stone castle on the shores of Lake Michigan, right in the center of town. It cost $80 million dollars in today's money.

The first Chicagoans to step inside the palace marveled at the interior, but they squinted at the artwork. Mrs. Palmer had decorated the walls with paintings she'd collected during her travels through France. But the paintings were so blurred and out of focus they made Chicagoans dizzy. Mrs. Palmer explained that these were the works of the "Impressionists"—Monet, Cezanne, Matisse, and Renoir. But the roughhewn Chicagoans just thought they weren't very good. Mrs. Palmer's tastes were somewhat ahead of her crowd.

Fermi Splits the Atom in the Squash Courts

At 3:25 P.M. on December 2, 1942, physicist Enrico Fermi and his colleagues split the atom. This Promethean feat—the first major step toward building the atomic bomb—took place in the squash courts under the west stand of the University of Chicago's Stagg Field. British sculptor Henry Moore memorialized the event with a bronze sculpture entitled Nuclear Energy. The artwork stands on the former squash site with a plaque that reads: "On December 2, 1942, man achieved here the first self-sustaining chain reaction and thereby initiated the controlled release of nuclear energy."

"Controlled release" is a bit misleading. As in any experiment, Fermi and crew made mistakes along the way, and the release of nuclear energy slipped slightly out of their control—a chilling foretaste of the future of nuclear power. The mistakes proved fatal. Twelve years later, Fermi died of cancer.

Students at the University of Chicago still claim that no matter how deep the snow gets in winter, Moore's sculpture is surrounded by a five-foot halo of snow-free earth.

The Melting Pot

When the Irish settled in Chicago during the last half of the nineteenth century, a network of Irish pubs fanned out across the most densely populated Irish neighborhoods. In the early days, these saloons served whiskey. But Chicago also had a large German population, and the Irish soon acquired a taste for the German beers. Soon the Irish saloons were serving more beer than whiskey.

Monkey Makeover

Maggie, the third oldest orangutan in North America, lives in Chicago's Brookfield Zoo. Until recently, the 43-year-old, 200-pound ape was overweight and had a cluster of health complaints: bad hair, dry skin, flatulence, and chronic snoring —all deadly to simian self-esteem. But after a University of Chicago endocrinologist diagnosed the ape with hypothyroidism, the zoo placed her on a high fiber diet. As a result, Maggie shed 90 pounds, her sleep improved, her snoring and flatulence abated, and her skin and hair regained a rich, luscious shimmer. The new sleeker Maggie is now dating a much younger man—Mukah, a 9-year-old ape.

Forever Young

When 29-year-old Julia Buccola Petta died in childbirth in 1921, she and her infant were buried in the same casket in Mt. Carmel Cemetery. Julia's mother had chronic nightmares about her daughter, until finally, years later, she insisted on having the coffin raised from the ground and opened. The infant had decomposed naturally, but the young mother was flawlessly preserved. Her family saw this as a miraculous event and took photographs. Today two photos of Julia, taken seven years apart—one in life and one in death—are affixed to the gravestone of "the Italian bride."

> *The infant had decomposed naturally, but the young mother was flawlessly preserved.*

Dial "O" for O'Malley

In the 1940s movies *The Bells of St. Mary's* and *Going My Way*, Bing Crosby plays a character named Father O'Malley. This character is allegedly based on Chicago's Father Eugene O'Malley who directed the famed Paulist Choir at Old St. Mary's Church, one of the city's oldest Catholic parishes, for half a century until 1968.

Time Capsule

Real estate mogul Donald Trump recently purchased the riverfront headquarters of the *Chicago Sun-Times* at 401 North Wabash as the future site of his Trump Towers. In October 2004, Trump began demolition of the old Sun-Times building, which Marshall Field III built in 1958.

On October 7, building engineers located a time capsule that Field had buried inside the structure during its construction. There were no records on the time capsule's location, but a longtime employee recalled how to find it. Field had designed the box to last 18,000 years, but his building lasted less than 50. With the approval of the *Sun-Times* top brass, excavators drilled open the time capsule 17,950 years early. It

> *Field had designed the box to last 18,000 years.*

contained the first edition of the *Chicago Sun* from December 4, 1941, with headlines describing Nazi troops advancing across Eastern Europe, a signed copy of Marshall Field III's book *Freedom is More Than a Word*, audio tapes of speeches from the building's dedication, and microfilm copies of the first editions of the *Chicago Sun, Chicago Times,* and *Chicago Sun-Times,* the latter dated February 2, 1958. The contents were considered somewhat disappointing. Excavators were hoping for a bottle of scotch.

Chicago is a vast outdoor museum of great architecture.

— Ira J. Bach

Hospital Founder Smuggles Chagall Out of France

When Chicago's Rehabilitation Institute opened its lakefront facility, they asked Marc Chagall to design a tapestry for the hospital's central foyer. In 1985, shortly before the tapestry was finished, Chagall died, and the French government banned the exportation of his work, while his family negotiated a settlement of the death duties. Undeterred, Dr. Henry Betts, the hospital's resourceful founder, rolled the tapestry in a rug and carried it out of France himself. It remains the centerpiece of the Institute and one of three Chagalls in Chicago.

It remained on the glass for more than 20 years, until a newsboy threw a paper through the window.

The Unwashable Window

April 18, 1924 remains frozen in the annals of the Chicago Fire Department. Francis X. Leavy, a young firefighter, climbed a ladder to wash the windows of the firehouse near 13th and Oakley, when an alarm sounded. Leavy rushed off to fight the blaze at 14th and Blue Island Avenue and perished when the building collapsed. Later, when another firefighter returned to finish the window Leavy had been working on, he could not scrub off Leavy's handprint. In fact, no one could remove it. It remained on the glass for more than twenty years, until a newsboy threw a paper through the window.

Sabotage or Espionage?

On December 8, 1972, a United Airlines 737 was about to land at Chicago's Midway, when it plunged into three neighborhood homes at the south end of the airport near 70th and Lawndale Avenue. The crash killed two neighborhood residents and 43 passengers and crewmembers. No one was able to explain why one of the casualties, Mrs. E. Howard Hunt, was traveling from Washington to Chicago with $10,000 in cash on her person. The next year, the Watergate Scandal forced President Richard M. Nixon to resign from office, and Howard Hunt went to prison for his role in the Watergate burglary and cover up.

Glowing in the Dark

During World War II, University of Chicago scientists labored on the Manhattan Project—the race to construct the first atomic bomb. After physicist Enrico Fermi and team split the atom, other scientists constructed the world's first nuclear reactor in Red Gate Woods, a 200-acre piece of Cook County Forest Preserve property in suburban Palos Hills. Nuclear debris was "buried" in the forest preserve. Visitors are cautioned not to do any digging. Most people avoid the site.

Activists Make Plans for the 1968 Democratic National Convention

In March 1968, the National Mobilization to End the War in Vietnam (MOBE) met at a YMCA camp near Chicago to plan demonstrations for the upcoming Democratic National Convention. Rennie Davis and Tom Hayden of MOBE were primarily interested in organizing nonviolent protests against the Vietnam War.

Abbie Hoffman and Jerry Rubin, founders of the Youth International Party (YIPPIES), were planning a different demonstration—a countercultural "Festival of Life." The Yippies were political pranksters, known for their wacky publicity stunts. In October 1967, they'd organized an "exorcism" of the Pentagon, in which 75,000 protestors encircled the building and chanted in hopes of making the massive structure levitate 300 feet, vibrate, and turn orange. In January 1968, they released "A STATEMENT FROM YIP," inviting celebrants to Chicago:

The Yippies were political pranksters, known for their wacky publicity stunts.

"Join us in Chicago in August for an international festival of youth, music, and theater. Rise up and abandon the creeping meatball! Come all you rebels, youth spirits, rock minstrels, truth-seekers, peacock-freaks, poets, barricade-jumpers, dancers, lovers and artists!

"It is summer. It is the last week in August, and the NATIONAL DEATH PARTY meets to bless Lyndon Johnson. We are there! There are 50,000 of us dancing in the streets, throbbing with amplifiers and harmony. We are making love in the parks. We are reading, singing, laughing, printing newspapers, groping, and making a mock convention, and celebrating the birth of FREE AMERICA in our own time.

"Everything will be free. Bring blankets, tents, draft-cards, body-paint, Mr. Leary's Cow, food to share, music, eager skin, and happiness. The threats of LBJ, Mayor Daley, and J. Edgar Freako will not stop us. We are coming! We are coming from all over the world!

"The life of the American spirit is being torn asunder by the forces of violence, decay, and the napalm-cancer fiend. We demand the Politics of Ecstasy! We are the delicate spores of the new fierceness that will change America. We will create our own reality, we are Free America! And we will not accept the false theater of the Death Convention.

"We will be in Chicago. Begin preparations now! Chicago is yours! Do it!"

As the convention approached, the Hoffman and Rubin proposed other, wilder plans. Rubin wanted to nominate Pigasus the Immortal, a pig, for president. In August, the Yippies distributed a program encouraging festival-goers to bring "sleeping bags, extra food, blankets, bottles of fireflies, cold cream, lots of handkerchiefs and canteens to deal with pig spray (1960s slang for tear gas), love beads, electric toothbrushes, see-through blouses, manifestos, magazines, and tenacity." The program also promised numerous activities, including meditation, poetry reading, rock bands, and "a dawn ass-washing ceremony." Other activities proved difficult to explain in court:

"Psychedelic long-haired mutant-jissomed peace leftists will consort with known dope fiends, spilling out onto the sidewalks in pornape disarray each afternoon . . . Two-hundred thirty rebel cocksmen under secret vows are on a 24-hour alert to get the pants of the daughters and wifes and kept women of the convention delegates."

In court, Hoffman claimed that he had written the program in fun and never intended it to be taken seriously.

University Rumors

Every college campus has its share of cruel and unusual hazing lore. University of Chicago students cringe at the tale of Ida Noyes, scion of a well-heeled family, who tried to make friends by joining a sorority. As part of the requisite hazing ritual, the sisters rowed Ida out on Lake Michigan, tossed her into the fifty-degree water, and promised to admit her if she swam to shore. Ida thrashed about, but she'd never learned to swim. Her dress filled with water and dragged her to the bottom of the lake before the sisters could fish her out. After the drowning, Ida's philanthropic father donated a building to the school in her memory, but the gift came with two stipulations: From now on, all U of C students must pass a swim test and no sorority may own a house on campus. The university has enforced these rules ever since.

According to the *University of Chicago* magazine, this tale is far from fact. In 1913, La Verne Noyes donated $300,000 to the University of Chicago in memory of his wife, Ida Elizabeth Smith Noyes, who had attended Iowa State College before she moved to Chicago with her husband. Noyes' funds went toward a "women's social center and gymnasium," but he didn't lay down any rules for swim tests or sororities. U of C sororities don't own houses because they can't afford to buy campus property, but the truth isn't intriguing enough to whet the students' appetite for gossip. According to another U of C fiction, the school lacks sorority houses because an antiquated state law defines a household of more than three women as a brothel.

The Lincolns' Ailments

People speak of the Kennedy curse, but the Lincolns had it worse. Abraham Lincoln was assassinated, three of his four sons died before reaching adulthood, and his widow, Mary Todd, was committed to a state hospital for the insane.

Not long after Lincoln's death, Mary settled in Chicago. Residents found her rather unusual. She carried her money in her undergarments. She also went on manic shopping binges, buying 84 pairs of kid gloves in less than a month.

In 1871, Mary was living in Chicago's Clifton Hotel with her 18-year-old son Tad, when Tad contracted a cold and died of compression of the heart and dropsy of the chest. She later moved into the Grand Pacific Hotel at Jackson and Clark with her son Robert. There, she roamed the hotel half-naked and sometimes used only candles for fear that gas was the devil's work. In 1875, she mistook the elevator for a bathroom and claimed Robert was trying to murder her, as hotel employees and her son dragged her back to her room. Robert reluctantly took out a warrant for her arrest. At her trial, the all-male jury took only ten minutes to commit her to an asylum. Mary Todd claimed that an Indian spirit was lifting her scalp off her head and pulling wires from her eyes, bones from her cheeks, and springs from her jaws. According to one doctor's bizarre diagnosis, Mary had too much blood in her brain, caused by attending séances to contact her dead husband and sons. After four months of confinement, Mary was released, but her ailments worsened. By 1882, she was also suffering from progressive spinal disease. Later that year, she died of a stroke.

In 1999, Norbert Hirschhorn and Robert Feldman reviewed Mrs. Lincoln's medical records and found that she was suffering from tabes dorsalis, a type of paralysis associated with tertiary syphilis. There is some speculation as to whether Mary Todd had syphilis, which could have caused her madness as well as her spinal condition. Abraham Lincoln apparently thought he had syphilis, though he was also known for hypochondria. (Fear of syphilis was not uncommon in his day, since an estimated 15 percent of the population was infected.) According to William Herndon, Lincoln's friend, biographer, and law partner, Lincoln believed he contracted the disease in 1835 or 1836. While in office, he took blue pills containing 65 milligrams of elemental mercury, a common treatment for syphilis before the discovery of penicillin.

One could determine whether the Lincolns had syphilis by testing their bones, but many Americans would probably rather not know. Lincoln has been voted America's most popular chief-of-state, and fans took umbrage when Gore Vidal claimed on NBC's *Today Show* and *Larry King Live* that Mary Todd got syphilis from her husband. As Jan Morris observed in *Lincoln: A Foreigner's Quest*, "the American people as a whole were almost deranged in their obsession with their sixteenth president."

One could determine whether the Lincolns had syphilis by testing their bones.

PART II:
Law & Disorder

Laws should be like clothes. They should fit the people they are meant to serve.

— Clarence Darrow

They blamed everything but the Chicago fire on me.

— Al Capone

Chicago strives to be the biggest and the best at everything, but when it comes to crime, Chicago doesn't have to try. From Al Capone to John Wayne Gacy, the place is crawling with crooks. If they gave out Grammies for dastardly deeds, Chicago would clean up.

Some convicts would win prizes for bizarre post-mortem spectacles. In 1882, death row inmate James Tracy donated his body to science. After his hanging, doctors tried to revive him with muscle-twitching, eye-opening jolts of electricity.

In the 1980s, "the Wimp" was buried at the wheel of a customized Cadillac Eldorado coffin with diamond rings glistening on every knuckle and crisp $1,000 bills between his fingers.

The award for comic lunacy goes to Butch, Pops, and Peanuts Panczko. In a whirlwind of crazed collective kleptomania, these three brothers stole everything from trucks to pedigree poodles and were arrested 214 times in 25 years. Keith Wheeler called the Panczko boys "pure, unduplicatable Chicago. . . they help explain why—in Chicago—it is unwise to take your eyes off any asset smaller than a locomotive."

Runner-ups include city building inspector Michael Moran, who impersonated a police officer to receive free car washes, and the infamous "Snowman," Salvatore Mucerino, who billed the City for snow removal services that he never performed.

Chicago also claims some of the smartest criminals. At 19, Nathan Leopold was the world's foremost expert on the Kirtland Warbler, knew 15 languages, and had been accepted at Harvard Law School, when he was arrested and convicted of the murder of Bobby Franks. Leopold had perhaps the highest recorded IQ of any US convict, testing at 210. Coming in a close second, with an alleged IQ of 200, is Al Capone. For those unimpressed with standardized test scores, there's "Handy Andy" Lowe, who never robbed a house without scouring the library and making scholarly annotations in the margins of his victims' books.

Victims claimed he displayed an unusually nuanced grasp of many disciplines. It was as if a band of professors had robbed them.

Some of the savviest lawbreakers are lawmakers. Aldermen Michael "Hinky Dink" Kenna and "Bathhouse" John Coughlin ran the First Ward for 40 years, controlling votes and doling out favors to the highest bidder. For the right price, they sold government jobs at city, state, and federal levels and guaranteed election results. Ballot-stuffing services ran from $8,000 to $100,000 per vote.

> *Ballot-stuffing services ran from $8,000 to $100,000 per vote.*

And who could forget the mayors who helped muscle some of America's best-loved presidents into office. Mayor Long John Wentworth ensured Abraham Lincoln's nomination at the 1860 Republican National Convention. Mayor Edward Kelley saw that the "Voice from the Sewer" sent FDR toward an unprecedented third term. Some say Mayor Richard Daley controlled the flow of Cook County votes to tip the scales in John F. Kennedy's favor. As they say in Chicago, "Vote early . . . vote often."

But the city isn't all scofflaws. It also produced Allan Pinkerton, the first private eye, Clarence Darrow, one of the nation's finest defense attorneys, and Officer Jack Muller, the only parking ticket cop who ever became a local hero.

"You're Fired"

In 1861, long before Donald Trump claimed these words as his personal soundbite, Mayor Long John Wentworth pink-slipped the entire Chicago Police Department. This was Wentworth's last official act before his mayoral term ended. It is not clear why he fired the entire force, but it was probably the result of a political squabble. Sixty officers, three sergeants, three lieutenants, and one captain lost their jobs. The city went copless, while a fresh force took their oaths. Twelve hours later, the CPD returned to the streets with an all-new cast.

Vice District

The South Side Levee, Chicago's vice district, rose during the 1893 World's Columbian Exposition, as millions of pleasure-seekers from around the globe flocked to the city. In the early 1900s, as the Levee grew and prospered, Chicago grandees like Potter Palmer fled the area for more auspicious places, such as North Lake Shore Drive. Prairie Avenue fell into disrepair, and in addition to providing illicit entertainments, the Levee spawned gangsters like Johnny Torrio and Al Capone.

From Big Jim Colosimo to Al Capone

If Al Capone is the father of gangland crime in Chicago, then James "Big Jim" Colosimo is the granddaddy. "Big Jim" ruled the "outfit," as the Chicago mafia was colloquially called, and presided over one of the Levee's three vice rings. He commandeered the street sweeper's union and had links to the Black Hand, a mafia-related crime society that flourished in late nineteenth-century Sicily and early 20th-century New York. An old-world bordello keeper, Colosimo operated two brothels with his wife and business partner, Victoria Moresco. They later opened a café at 2126 South Wabash Avenue that drew an illustrious clientele, including Potter Palmer, Marshall Field, Enrico Caruso, Al Jolson, Clarence Darrow, and George M. Cohan. Big Jim wore diamond rings on every finger and diamond-studded belts. He hobnobbed with the Chicago elite. No one cared that he was a pimp. His café stayed open for most of Prohibition (it was shut down only twice).

> *Big Jim wore diamond rings on every finger and diamond-studded belts.*

As Big Jim entered his café on the morning of May 11, 1920, an unidentified gunman stepped out of the cloakroom and gunned him down. Three judges and nine aldermen served as pallbearers at his funeral. Mike "The Greek" Potson, a former Indiana barkeep, took over Big Jim's café, but Colosimo's successor was his nephew and right-hand man, Johnny Torrio, the gangland mentor of Al Capone. Colosimo had imported the discreet, shrewd Torrio from New York to build his business. A pioneer in modern crime, Torrio refashioned racketeering, giving it a corporate structure.

While living an outwardly respectable life, he took the first steps in transforming an Italian feudal crime society into a modern corporate enterprise. Capone carried this to new heights.

Alphonse Capone was born in Brooklyn in 1899. His father was literate, made more money than most Italian immigrants, and wasn't involved in the mafia. At age ten, Al started running errands for Torrio, his idol. Later he joined the Five Pointers gang in Manhattan's Lower East Side. In 1919, Torrio offered Capone a job at his Four Deuces Club at 2222 South Wabash in Chicago. Al left his respectable bookkeeping job in Baltimore and came to work for his idol. He got his start mopping floors for $25 a week and standing outside the club inviting passersby to visit the bordello on the fourth floor. A few months later, he was earning $75 a week as a bouncer for the club and Torrio's bodyguard.

In 1925, Torrio barely survived an attempt on his life. Before returning to Italy, he crowned "Big Al" mob boss.

Saint Valentine's Day Massacre

Throughout Prohibition, rival mobsters competed for the bootleg liquor trade. In 1929, Al Capone's henchman, Machine Gun McGurn assembled a team of gangsters from out of town and hatched an imaginative plan to assassinate Bugs Moran, the boss of the rival Moran gang. No one thought the hit would be remembered for decades to come.

A bootlegger lured the Moran gang to a garage at 2122 North Clark Street to buy some moonshine at bargain rates. The delivery was scheduled for 10:30 A.M. on February 14, 1929. When the Moran gang showed up, McGurn's team pulled up to the garage in a stolen police car and staged a mock raid. Dressed in police uniforms and trench coats, they ordered the bootleggers to line up against the wall. When the gangsters lined up as told, the four hit men stripped them of their guns and opened fire.

To make their getaway, the two hit men in trench coats walked out of the garage with their hands up, followed by two uniformed police officers, so any witnesses would believe they'd seen two cops arresting two bootleggers. The team left the scene in the police car. The ambush went as planned, except the main target, Bugs Moran, survived the slaughter because he was late to the meeting. When he saw the cops pull up, he took off.

> When the gangsters lined up as told, the four hit men stripped them of their guns and opened fire.

Everyone in Chicago knew Capone and McGurn had engineered the attempt on Bugs' life. But Capone was in Florida, and McGurn was in a hotel room with his girlfriend, Louise Rolfe. Machine Gun married his "blond alibi" after the massacre so she could not testify against him. No one was tried for the murders, even though everyone knew who was responsible.

The "Saint Valentines Day Massacre" attracted more publicity than any prior mob crime. It became synonymous with the violence of the Roaring Twenties and made Capone into a national celebrity. Writers nationwide churned out articles and books on him. As Laurence Bergreen, author of *Capone: The Man and The Time*, wrote, "There had never been an outlaw quite like Al Capone. He was elegant, high-class, the berries. He was remarkably brazen, continuing to live among the swells in Miami and to proclaim love for his family. Nor did he project the image of a misfit or a loner, he played the part of a self-made millionaire who could show those Wall Street big shots a thing or two about doing business in America. No one was indifferent to Capone; everyone had an opinion about him."

But while the massacre made Capone famous, it also made him a wanted man. He continued to live in a lavish display of wealth, as if he didn't realize he was public enemy number one. President Herbert Hoover pressured Treasury Secretary Andrew Mellon to gather evidence of income tax evasion. In May 1929, Capone was arrested outside a Philadelphia movie house for tax fraud and carrying a concealed weapon. Capone's business card said he was a used furniture dealer.

Chicagoans Inspire the Mann Act

Maurice and Julia Van Bever, a married couple, controlled another of the Levee vice rings. They presided over an interstate prostitution ring from St. Louis to Chicago. Charley Maibum, who controlled the Levee's third vice ring, owned a "pay by the hour" inn where streetwalkers brought their customers for quick tricks.

Before 1910, brothel keepers had little trouble paying police and politicians to look the other way. The authorities were less tolerant of procuring (in other words, they required the procurers to dig deeper in their pockets for that).

The Van Bevers inspired the legendary Mann Act, also known as the "White Slavery Act," of 1910. Representative James Robert Mann of Illinois introduced the act, which prohibited the transportation of women across state lines for immoral purposes. But the Van Bever's business wasn't simply interstate. They allegedly imported more than 20,000 women into the U.S. to staff their bordellos.

Buns of Steel

In 2004, Officer Frederico Andaverde, 34, received Chicago's top police honor, the Lambert Tree Award. He also earned a new nickname, when he and his partner, Officer Andrew J. Dakuras, got caught in a gun battle with two criminals, whom they subsequently arrested. During the shootout, a 9-mm bullet sliced through the door of the unmarked police car and perforated Andaverde's back pocket, his wallet, his credit cards and his HMO card. The bullet stopped just short of his skin. Before Andaverde could return to his station, friends called making reference to his "buns of steel." He continues to receive copies of the video by that name in the mail.

Of course, we know it was his credit cards and HMO card that saved him. Who says those HMOs don't offer protection?

The Singing Burglar

Petty thief Richard Morrison is remembered as the "singing burglar." His "song" caused quite a stir in the Chicago Police Department. It triggered the worst scandal in the department's history. In the late 1950s, the cops caught Morrison red-handed and questioned him. Pressured to name his accomplices, Morrison gained immortality in Chicago by "singing," divulging some 77 pages of testimony on his strategists, lookouts, fellow thieves, and reconnaissance patrols who combed through stores and unlocked doors to aid his robberies. These accomplices all turned out to be officers from the Chicago Police Department's Summerdale District. This led to a thorough housecleaning of Chicago law enforcement, and the city hired Orlando Wilson, its first civilian police commissioner from out of town.

O'Hare's History

Chicago's O'Hare international airport is named for Lieutenant Commander Edward J. O'Hare. President Franklin Delano Roosevelt awarded this Chicagoan a Congressional Medal of Honor in World War II. O'Hare flew against the Imperial Air Force of Japan virtually single handed, thus protecting the USS Lexington, the one remaining aircraft carrier in the Pacific Fleet.

After receiving the medal, O'Hare, who had movie star good looks, was sent across the U.S. as a poster boy for the war effort. But he insisted on returning to active duty and later perished on a naval aviation mission in the Pacific.

O'Hare graduated from the U.S. Naval Academy at Annapolis. But few Chicagoans know that he got into this academy only after his own father, attorney Edward J. O'Hare, Sr., went undercover and became an inside informer on Al Capone's mob. O'Hare Senior's privileged position within the crime organization helped put Capone in prison following his conviction on tax evasion charges. But when O'Hare agreed to spy on Capone, he made a deal. He would go undercover only if the feds guaranteed his son's lifelong dream—an appointment to the U.S. Naval Academy.

O'Hare Senior never lived to see his son's military fame. He was gunned down in November of 1939 on Chicago's Ogden Avenue while returning from Sportsman's Park, a local racetrack connected to the Capone mob.

The Parking Cop Who Did His Job

Naval officer Jack Muller joined the Chicago Police Department after serving in World War II. After seeing combat, writing parking violations was a piece of cake.

The strange thing about Muller was that he spared no one. In a city built on inside connections, nods and winks, this stands out. Over the years, he ticketed the cars of Mayor Richard J. Daley, Illinois Governor William G. Stratton, Cook County Board President Dan Ryan, and even neighboring Gary, Indiana Mayor Richard Hatcher. Whether

The strange thing was that he spared no one.

outside City Hall or the Rush Street nightclubs, where the management slipped beat cops $100 to stay away from customers' cars, Muller treated everyone the same. He even tucked a ticket under the windshield-wipers of mob boss Tony "Big Tuna" Accardo's fancy sedan.

Elegant Vice

Sisters Ada and Minna Everleigh were two of Chicago's leading entrepreneurs at the turn of the 20th century. In 1900, they opened the Everleigh Club at 2131–3 South Dearborn Street and distributed brochures throughout the Midwest. Visitors came from around the globe to partake of the high-class goings-on that the Everleigh sisters offered only to the most discerning gentlemen.

The Everleigh sisters hired porters, servants, and chefs to staff the six parlors and 50 bedrooms, richly groomed with tapestries and Impressionist paintings. Orchestras played in the drawing rooms. A gold piano stood in the Gold Room, along with gold-rimmed fishbowls and gold spittoons. And the Everleighs employed only the most refined, cultured women and supplied a library so they could continue their studies.

This was no ordinary run-of-the-mill whorehouse. This was high-class entertainment that cost up to $500 a night. Here the commercial titans and captains of U.S. industry might pay a discrete visit. Politicians and businessmen whose names had instant social caché roamed the approximately 50 rooms of the Everleigh mansion. Such goings-on can generate vicious gossip. When 37-year-old Marshall Field, Jr. was found dead in his bedroom at 1919 South Prairie Avenue, his family claimed he had accidentally shot himself in the stomach while dressing to go hunting. But rumors spread that he was shot at the Everleigh Club and smuggled home to avoid police inquiry and press sensations.

The Everleigh girls had friends in high places, and the very highest were the two aldermen in whose ward the sisters operated their enterprise—Michael "Hinky Dink" Kenna and "Bathhouse" John Coughlin. The sisters enjoyed remarkable success until Chicago reformers organized an anti-vice crusade. When Carter Harrison II was elected mayor, he ordered Captain Patrick J. Harding to shut down the operation. At first, the captain ignored the order. After all, the Everleighs paid high prices for police protection. When the mayor repeated the order, Harding paid a visit to Hinky Dink and Bathhouse, the aldermen of the First Ward. The captain did nothing until he obtained a go-ahead from these "lords of the levee." But in 1911, the place was finally padlocked, and the wealthy sisters moved to the city's west side and later to New York, after their Chicago neighbor made a fuss. In 1933, the club was torn down. A public housing project called the Hillard Homes now stands in its place.

The fall of Everleigh in 1911 cracked Democratic political alliances. Kenna and Coughlin turned on the mayor and eventually defeated him at the polls. Republican William Hale "Big Bill" Thompson stepped into the vacuum, and his administration was so corrupt that many people thought the mob was payrolling him. In fact, Al Capone was among the largest contributors to Big Bill's campaign. The gangster hung portraits of George Washington, Abraham Lincoln, and Big Bill Thompson behind his desk at his Lexington Hotel headquarters.

Lords of the Levee

From 1897 to 1938, aldermen Michael "Hinky Dink" Kenna and "Bathhouse" John Coughlin ran the First Ward. "Bathhouse," a large man who once worked as a masseur in a Turkish bath, wore garish waistcoats and spouted bad poetry at city council meetings. His poems often concerned civic matters, as evidenced by their titles: "She Sleeps by the Drainage Canal," "They're Tearing Up Clark Street Again," and "Why Did They Build the Lovely Lake So Close to the Horrible Shore?" It turned out that *Chicago Tribune* reporter John Kelley had actually penned many of Coughlin's poems, though Coughlin had no problem taking credit for them. When Mayor Harrison asked Kenna if Coughlin was crazy or drugged, Kenna said neither, but, "To tell you the god's truth, Mayor, they ain't found a name for it yet."

In contrast to Coughlin, Hinky Dink Kenna was small, shrewd, and tight-lipped. He owned the Workingman's Exchange on Clark Street, which served free lunch and the "Largest and Coolest Schooner of Beer in the City." For more than 20 years, Kenna fed the homeless and jobless for a nickel. He also found them work and helped those in trouble with the law.

While this may sound like a humanitarian enterprise, Hinky Dink also told his clientele how to vote, and he didn't lose an election in 40 years. Each election day, Coughlin and Kenna marshaled the First Ward party workers to rouse the bums sleeping on the streets and herd them to a polling place, where they received marked ballots to deposit in a box. For a little extra cash, they could swipe unmarked ballots and sell them to Coughlin and Kenna's helpers for 50 cents to a dollar. These ballots were marked, given to another round of tramps and so on.

Coughlin and Kenna grew rich doling out favors to the highest bidder. In addition to guaranteed votes, they offered protection for illicit business ventures. Their weekly tithes ranged from $25 for small brothels to $100 for large ones, plus additional fees for liquor and gambling. For fees of $500 to $2,000, they saw to it that charges of theft, kidnapping, pandering or grand larceny were dropped. They could provide these amenities because someone in virtually every government office in Chicago owed them favors. Coughlin and Kenna controlled most city jobs, including police jobs. Their graft practices brought in $15,000 to $30,000 per year, though their ballot-stuffing services ran anywhere from $8,000 to $100,000 per vote.

> *Their graft practices brought in $15,000 to $30,000 per year.*

Annual Underworld Orgy

Chicago's underworld ball tradition began around 1880 with a charity event for Lame Jimmy, a pianist who worked for madam Carrie Watson. These parties were shut down in 1895, after a drunken detective shot another cop at the charity gathering.

Hinky Dink Kenna and Bathhouse Coughlin, elected First Ward aldermen in 1897, decided to revive the custom. But Coughlin and Kenna's annual First Ward Ball was a mandatory event. Every prostitute, pickpocket and thief had to purchase a ticket. Brothel and saloonkeepers had to buy them in bulk. City officials and madams reserved their own boxes. The ball, dubbed the "annual underworld orgy," took place at the Chicago Coliseum. Each party raked in about $50,000 for Coughlin and Kenna. Following one debacle, the *Tribune* reported, "If a great disaster had befallen the Coliseum last night, there would not have been a second story worker, a dip or pug ugly, porch climber, dope fiend or scarlet woman remaining in Chicago."

Women who fainted were lifted up and passed over people's heads toward the exits.

The 1907 ball received the widest press coverage and thus fanned the ire of anti-vice crusaders. That year, 15,000 guests crammed the Coliseum so tightly that drunks who passed out could not even fall to the floor. Women who fainted were lifted up and passed over people's heads toward the exits. At the opening of the debauch, Bathhouse John in a red sash and lavender cravat led a promenade of First Ward prostitutes into the

Coliseum. Chicago journalists Lloyd Wendt and Herman Kogan wrote, "On they came, madams, strumpets, airily clad jockeys, harlequins, Diana's, page boys, female impersonators, tramps, pan handlers, card sharps, mountebanks, pimps, owners of dives and resorts, young bloods and 'older men careless of their reputations.'" Women leaned backward over railings and commanded men to pour champagne down their throats. "The girls in peekaboo waists, slit skirts, bathing suits and jockey costumes relaxed and tripped to the floor where they danced wildly and drunkenly . . . drunken men sought to undress young women and met with few objections." The newspapers also mentioned "drag queens" in attendance which made anti-vice reformers particularly irate.

The Chicago police sent 100 officers to the ball, but they made only eight arrests, resulting in one conviction—Barnard Dooley was fined for sneaking into the debacle without paying.

After the 1907 press coverage, reformers demanded the debauch be shut down. Grace Episcopal Church took the matter to the Superior Court, which simply stated that the event was not in its jurisdiction. Two days before the 1908 ball, a bomb went off in the Coliseum. The explosion—the work of "radical reformers" according to police—wrecked a two-story warehouse and shattered windows two blocks away. But the event went on as usual. Bathhouse John said it was "the nicest Derby we ever had." But Reverend Melbourne P. Boynton of the Lexington Avenue Baptist Church found it "unspeakable low, vulgar and immoral," and in 1909, the anti-vice campaigners made such a fuss that Mayor Fred Busse denied the ball a liquor license, and the First Ward Ball ground to a sad halt.

Sperm Wars

Dr. Richard O. Phillips has been suing Dr. Sharon Irons for deception, while paying $800 a month to support their five-year-old daughter. Irons manually inseminated herself with Phillips' sperm during a brief affair six years ago in Chicago. Though a judge dismissed Phillips' claims of deception, an Illinois Appeals Court partially reversed the decision, calling for a trial to decide if Irons inflicted "emotional distress" on Phillips. But in response to Phillips' claim that Irons stole his sperm, the court ruled, "it was a gift, an absolute and irrevocable transfer of title to property from a donor to a donee." Since there was no agreement to return the gift, Irons was entitled to do as she pleased with it.

Memory Loss

In 1899, Chicago Alderman Michael "Hinky Dink" Kenna appeared before a committee investigating corruption in Chicago. His First Ward, long known as the city's center of gambling and prostitution, was under investigation. The committee grilled Kenna, pressuring him to reveal the names of people who patronized such establishments. Hinky Dink refused to betray his friends. He testified that he could not recall a single name. The interrogation could barely proceed due to spectators' laughter.

Leopold and Loeb

In May 1924, a laborer found the body of 14-year-old Bobby Franks, scion of a prominent Chicago family, in a marshland near the Indiana border. The only concrete clue was a pair of horn-rimmed glasses found with the body. The spectacles had an odd hinge, which the police traced to one optometrist, who linked the prescription to Nathan Leopold, 19, the son of a box-manufacturing millionaire.

He was also obsessed with Richard Loeb, 18, who was in turn obsessed with crime.

A brilliant student, Leopold was already the world's foremost expert on an endangered songbird, the Kirtland Warbler. Clarence Darrow wrote in his 1932 autobiography that Leopold "had, and has, the most brilliant intellect that I ever met in a boy." He had scored a remarkable 210 on an IQ test. At age 19, he was studying law at the University of Chicago and matriculating to Harvard Law

School in the fall. He was also obsessed with Richard Loeb, 18, who was in turn obsessed with crime. Loeb, who also came from a privileged background, was entranced with the idea of committing the perfect crime. In some ways he fit the profile of a psychopath—he saw the kidnapping and murder of Bobby Franks as an escape from the quotidian, an intellectual exercise. Leopold claimed that his motive "to the extent that I had one, was to please Dick."

The boys spent hours hatching their plan to abduct a child and demand that the parents throw ransom money off a moving train at a designated location. The murder, they claimed, was not enjoyable but necessary to reduce the likelihood that they would be identified as the kidnappers.

Their "perfect crime" went awry. Before Franks' father left home with the ransom, a laborer discovered Franks' body. The glasses, found near the victim, led the cops to Leopold, who led them to Loeb. The two boys confessed to the kidnapping, but each claimed the other was the killer.

Their parents hired Darrow to save their sons from the gallows. At first, Leopold looked down on Darrow with his wild hair, rumpled, egg-splattered suit and crooked tie, but his opinion quickly changed. Darrow changed the boys' pleas from "not guilty (by reason of insanity) to "guilty." This meant that the judge rather than the jury would decide the sentence. In his summation, Darrow took the courtroom on a 12-hour oratorical rollercoaster, which would be unimaginable in a trial today. He based his criminal defense on a philosophy of determinism: "In the words of Omar Khayyam, we are only impotent pieces in the game He plays upon this checkerboard of nights and days . . . What had this boy to do with it? . . . He did not make himself. And yet he is to be compelled to pay."

Judge John R. Caverly sentenced the two boys to life imprisonment. Immediately after the trial, he and his

Darrow took the courtroom on a 12-hour oratorical rollercoaster.

wife checked themselves into a local hospital to recover. When Caverly returned to the bench, he refused to hear anything but divorce cases. "My health has been sapped," he said.

Aftermath of the "Trial of the Century"

Nathan Leopold and Richard Loeb were model prisoners, just as they were model students before they murdered Bobby Franks. In prison they opened a school for inmates and showed many signs of rehabilitation. Leopold remained infatuated with and devoted to Loeb, even though their relationship, as Leopold wrote in retrospect, "had cost me my life." He also called Loeb "a living contradiction." While Loeb "truly, deeply wanted to help his fellow man," he "didn't have the faintest trace of conventional morality" and never "felt truly remorseful for what we had done."

On January 28, 1936, Loeb's cellmate, James Day, attacked him with a straight razor in the shower. Loeb died of blood loss and shock. Day claimed he had assaulted Loeb in "self-defense," after Loeb made sexual advances toward him in the shower. The jury apparently saw this as a justifiable reason for murder. They found Day not guilty despite the facts—it was evident that Day had slashed Loeb's throat from behind, and Loeb had 58 wounds while Day had none. Most likely Day suspected that Loeb was shortchanging him on the cigarettes and candy that Loeb bought and gave out to his fellow inmates, but this explanation wouldn't have served Day as well in court. Based on Day's version of events, reporter Ed Lahey wrote a clever lead for the *Chicago Daily News*: "Richard Loeb, despite his erudition, today ended his sentence with a proposition."

Leopold lived until 1971. He spent the rest of his life helping others to expiate his crime. He also learned 13 languages while in prison (in addition to the 15 he already knew at age 19). After his release in 1958, he moved to Puerto Rico where he pursued his passion for ornithology, taught mathematics, and worked as an x-ray technician. He also married, though he insisted that he was still in love with Richard Loeb.

Loopy Laws

Visitors to Chicago, beware! You may have to take some unusual precautions to avoid arrest. Some of the following laws are still on the books:

- In Chicago, you may not take a French poodle to the opera. (Take your Great Dane to the opera. If the poodle complains, buy her tickets to the ballet.)
- It is against the law to offer a lighted cigar to a dog, cat, or other domestic pet.
- It is illegal to give a canine whiskey. (Most dogs prefer vodka anyway, and you can get a cat drunk on whatever you want.)
- An Oak Park ordinance forbids roosters from crowing before 6 A.M. (But are clocks displayed where the roosters might see them?)
- Before addressing a man in Chicago, be sure to ask if he's married. He may think this is a pickup line, but it is actually a legal precaution. According to penal code, the proper title for a bachelor is "Master" rather than "Mister."
- A man may not fish in his pajamas. (Clearly gender discrimination's at work here.)
- In Chicago, anyone carrying less than one dollar on her person may be arrested for vagrancy.

Lager Beer Riots

The Lager Beer Riots of April 21, 1855 remain a blemish on Chicago's history. The city's mayor was Levi Boone, a descendent of frontiersman Daniel Boone and a member of the Know Nothing Party, a white supremacist and anti-immigrant organization. Boone closed the German beer halls on Sundays, the only day the city's German residents could socialize and relax. Led by an army of saloonkeepers, the outraged Germans organized and marched from their northside neighborhoods to City Hall. Boone summoned a militia of some 150 special deputies to stamp out the protest. Under the mayor's orders, they swung the Clark Street Bridge, making it impossible for the German marchers to cross. Boone also had Chicago police sharpshooters conceal themselves in the upper portions of the bridge and open fire on the German marchers as they neared the river's edge. The fusillade left many dead and even more injured. Chicagoans had the last word on Mayor Boone at the polls. He lost the next election, only weeks later.

Anton J. Cermak

Anton J. Cermak, born in Bohemia, then part of the Austro-Hungarian Empire, became Chicago's first and only immigrant mayor in 1931. Though a Democrat, Cermak was no fan of Franklin Delano Roosevelt when he ran for president in 1933. At the advice of party insiders, Roosevelt reached out to Cermak and invited him to Florida for the presidential inauguration. Cermak joined the president-elect in Miami and sat at his side as the motorcade drove to a special rally on February 15, 1933. As the motorcade pulled up to the stage, shots rang out. Cermak and five bystanders were wounded by bullets from the gun of Giuseppe Zangara, an Italian immigrant who was—supposedly—aiming at Roosevelt. Within 14 days, Zangara was tried and convicted on six counts of attempted murder. Cermak rallied in a Miami hospital, but within weeks his condition worsened. He died on March 6, 1933. The autopsy revealed that portions of the bullet had perforated his bowel, and Cermak died of peritonitis. Within hours, Zangara was back in court facing a murder charge. He was convicted and executed almost immediately.

> As the motorcade pulled up to the stage, shots rang out.

   While most historians interpret the shooting as an attempt at Roosevelt's life, some Chicago residents have a different view. Before Roosevelt's inauguration, Frank Nitti, the thug who ran the Capone Empire while "Big Al" was in prison, tried to assassinate Cermak. The mayor's bodyguards shot Nitti, but he survived and put out a "hit" on Cermak. Some think that the mafia was holding Zangara's family hostage back in Italy and offered to free them if he shot the mayor. Chicago was still a gangland fief in the grips of the final months of prohibition.

Brunch Ban

With the start of the 2004 Chicago Bears football season, restaurant owners are requesting permission to open bars earlier—at 10 A.M. instead of 11. Bears fans say they need to start winding up for the games earlier, and restaurants want to accommodate them. Tailgaters in the parking lots of Soldier Field, the Bears' home, begin their "brunch" preparations as early as 9 A.M. But, according to law, business owners who serve liquor have to wait until 11. All 6,700 Chicago saloon keepers and restaurant owners are asking aldermen to let them open earlier during professional football's brief season.

Dillinger Found Innocent 70 Years Too Late

In 1934, the infamous "Lady in Red" betrayed John Dillinger, Chicago's "public enemy number one," in front of a movie theater. But recently things have been looking up for Dillinger. In 2004, law enforcement officials in Green Bay, Wisconsin cleared him of the 1931 robbery of the South State Bank, where a gun battle left three policemen wounded. Apparently, Dillinger was in prison at the time of the crime. But he was released in time to take a volley of police bullets beside the Biograph Theater at Lincoln and Fullerton.

Crime Takes a Holiday

October 4, 2004 marked the first time that no homicides were reported. Chicago police announced the first 33 hours of peace. Police Superintendent Phil Cline noted that this was the first time in his 34 years on the force that he can recall a day with no murders. The Chicago Police homicide log remained empty for two days.

Vicious Cycle

A Chicago newspaper dubbed July through September 2004 "Vicious Cycle," because Chicago witnessed 19 motorcycle deaths during these months. While almost all U.S. states and European Union countries require motorcyclists to wear protective headgear, the State of Illinois has no such law. Chicago motorcyclists have long treasured this unheard of legal laxity. Legislators are busy crafting an ordinance requiring helmets.

Murder Most Foul

The name John Wayne Gacy still chills Chicagoans who remember the macabre reports of his bizarre 1978 killing spree. Though the clues pointed to Gacy, police were shocked when they entered his suburban home, smelled the grisly odors and found the bodies of his victims stashed in the crawl space of his house. Gacy, who targeted gay hustlers and other young men, was convicted of 33 murders—

more than anyone else in US history. In 1995, he was executed in an Illinois prison, after receiving 21 life terms and 12 death sentences for his crimes. Before his prison sentence, Gacy entertained kids at birthday parties as Pogo the party clown.

Never trust a woman or an automatic pistol.

— Bank robber John Dillinger

Gangland Scars

The Holy Name Cathedral on North State Street also bears traces of 1920s violence. The church, which opened in 1874, was one of the first public structures built in the aftermath of the Great Fire of 1871. It is made of a peculiar Illinois limestone, the same material as the Chicago Water Tower (the only structure that didn't perish in the fire's path). To many citizens, the neo-gothic church with soaring towers embodies the city's spirited recovery.

Irish gangster Dion O'Banion of the Bugs Moran gang ran a florist shop across the street from the cathedral. In October 1926—less than three years before the St. Valentine's Day Massacre—O'Banion's pal, mafia hit man Hymie Weiss, was gunned down in a volley of machine gun fire. The cornerstones of Holy Name Cathedral took the brunt of the machine-gun markings, and they still wear the scars.

More Loopy Laws

- Municipal law forbids flying a kite within city limits. Mayor Richard Daley nonetheless sponsors an annual "Kids and Kites Fest" in flagrant violation of the city code.

- It is illegal to eat in a burning building. If you try to do so, you not only risk asphyxiation, but arrest.

- It is legal for people 17 and under to protest naked in front of City Hall offices. (For those over 18, forget it. Look what the police did to the naked protestors at the 1968 Democratic National Convention.)

- Motorists are required by law to inform the Chicago Police Department before entering the city in an automobile.

- It is illegal to carry a switchblade in Chicago. While this isn't so odd, the same law bans hatpins, which are seen as concealed weapons.

- Only an officer of the law may use a slingshot in Chicago.

- Due to some misguided patriotism, it is illegal to speak English in the state of Illinois. You may only speak American. Brits must take care not to open their mouths around a police officer.

- Political correctness has its problems, but consider the alternatives. An early municipal law referred to citizens with physical deformities, skin disorders, and amputated limbs as "unsightly or disgusting objects" and forbade them to show their faces in public.

Machine Gun McGurn

"Machine Gun" Jack McGurn, denizen of the 1920s Chicago underworld and Capone henchman of the toughest order, probably masterminded the 1929 St. Valentine's Day Massacre. Chicagoans saw his fingerprints all over the slaughter of seven members of the rival Moran Gang, but police found little concrete evidence that McGurn had pulled the trigger. McGurn's crime caught up with him seven years later. On February 15, 1936, he was gunned down in a Chicago bowling alley on Milwaukee Avenue. Before fleeing the scene, the gunman pinned a Valentine to McGurn's body. It read:

You've lost your job,
You've lost your dough,
Your jewels and handsome houses,
But things could be worse, you know,
You haven't lost your trousers.

Murder for Hire

In the late 1880s, Chicago, like other Irish strongholds in the U.S. was a hotbed of revolutionary activity, aimed on achieving national independence for Ireland. In Chicago, bitter internal conflicts fractured Irish Americans into sects. The Clan-a-Gael, a secret army of volunteer rebels, advocated the armed overthrow of British rule. Dr. Patrick Henry Cronin, a Chicago physician and a powerful ally of

Parnell, incurred the wrath of the Chicago Clan. At the height of the conflict, Cronin disappeared. As Chicago police sought his whereabouts, rumors circulated that he had fled to Canada and was embarking on a secret trip to Ireland. Friends expressed skepticism, and their worse fears were realized when the doctor, or at least parts of him, showed up in Chicago. A number of body part were discovered in a storm drain on the city's Northside, near the Swedish neighborhood of Andersonville. Portions of his torso and head turned up in a trunk found floating near Montrose Harbor on the city's lakefront. Evidence on the trunk led police to a small group of dissident members of the Clan, long known for their hatred of Cronin. Witnesses identified the owner of the trunk, and arrests ensued.

As it turned out, Cronin's enemies had paid local hit men to do their bidding. It was Chicago's first murder for hire. Within months, the population of Chicago doubled when surrounding villages annexed themselves to the city, citing the added protection of municipal police as a chief reason. In Ireland, Parnell's struggle for home rule dissolved due to his relationship with another man's wife. The dream of Irish independence waited for another quarter century.

> As it turned out, Cronin's enemies had paid local hit men to do their bidding. It was Chicago's first murder for hire.

Tattletale Fingerprints

In the annals of Cook County justice, the 1912 trial of Thomas Jennings marks the first instance when fingerprints were admitted into court as evidence and used to obtain a murder conviction. The judge sentenced the defendant to death, and his execution set another, more grisly record. Jennings was the fifth convict hanged in the U.S. on February 16, 1912. No day has witnessed more executions in U.S. history.

Grandma's No Gun Moll

The Montana family, like many others in the Taylor Street Italian community, braved Prohibition by concocting their own booze. They enjoyed a thriving business until the cops showed up. As police climbed the front stairs, shots rang out, killing one officer. The assailant was none other than Grandma Montana, whose sharpshooting made her a neighborhood legend.

Lived to Tell

By 1983, Korean mob boss Ken Eto, had outworn his welcome among his gangster peers. As the FBI intensified efforts to break up the mob, Eto became a serious liability. Cohorts suspected he was on the edge of talking. It was no surprise when two gunmen confronted him near a Chicago movie theater and pumped three bullets into his head. The shocker was that he survived and served as an invaluable witness for the feds. His assassins met a much worse end. Their bodies turned up in a trunk in an apartment complex.

Marx Brothers of Crime

The "crime family" is a well-known Chicago phenomenon. But most mobster "families" were bonded by blood oaths, not blood. The Panczko boys—Butch, Pops and Peanuts—were real-life brother burglars. Joseph "Pops" Panczko found his vocation in 1930 at age 12. The brains of the family operation, he helped his younger brothers, Eddie "Butch" and Paul "Peanuts," develop their talents. During their 60-year crime career, they succeeded in every conceivable contortion of thievery—jimmying locks, stealing cars, picking pockets, pilfering booze, hijacking trucks, swiping chinchilla furs, and kidnapping pedigree poodles. Robbing everyone from jewelers to TV salesmen, they fooled most of the people most of the time.

The buffoons of burglary, the Panczko boys got arrested 214 times in 25 years.

The buffoons of burglary, the Panczko boys got arrested 214 times in 25 years. Keith Wheeler remarked, "They are pure, unduplicatable Chicago... they help explain why—in Chicago—it is unwise to take your eyes off any asset smaller than a locomotive."

Political Ambition

Eugene Patrick Prendergast sold newspapers from a stall in downtown Chicago near the city's municipal offices. He got involved in politics, lobbying for improvements in Chicago's level railroad crossings, and in 1893, he supported Mayor Carter Harrison's campaign for reelection. The deluded Prendergast expected Harrison to appoint him Corporation Counsel, the city's chief attorney. But Prendergast had never finished grade school and was totally unqualified for the position. When the mayor tapped someone else for the job, Prendergast flew into furious action. On October 28, 1893, just two days before the close of the World's Columbian Exposition, he presented himself at the office of the new Corporation Counsel and demanded that he resign from Prendergast's rightful post.

The startled lawyer assured Prendergast that he would resign on the spot. This white lie gave him the opportunity to escape from the crazed Prendergast. When he returned with the police, they saw Prendergast run through the lobby of City Hall and vanish into the crowd. He dashed all the way to Mayor Harrison's home on stately Ashland Avenue, rang the doorbell, and announced he had urgent business with Harrison. The mayor had no idea who Prendergast was, but the servants ushered him into the mayor's parlor. Prendergast shot the mayor in the head and fled the scene. He later turned himself in at a nearby police station.

Chicago plunged into shock, as the eve of the World Fair turned into a memorial for the mayor. Prendergast was convicted of murder and sentenced to die, even though the evidence indicated that he was out of his mind. At that time there was no provision for an insanity plea. Following his conviction, his family hired a young lawyer who argued that Prendergast should be spared the gallows due to insanity. The plea failed. Prendergast hanged in 1894. But the young lawyer, Clarence Darrow, went on to make a name for himself in Chicago and nationwide.

Unsolved Murders

In the summer of 1957, fifteen-year-old Judith Mae Anderson disappeared on her way home from a friend's house. Her dismembered body was found floating in the 50-gallon oil drums in Montrose Harbor. She was the sixth young person murdered in two years.

The naked bodies of the Grime sisters, 13 and 15, had turned up in January 1957, and in 1955, the naked bodies of three boys had been found in a forest preserve on the city's edge. No one was ever apprehended in the murders of Anderson or the Grimes sisters, but more than 40 years later, a man was convicted of the murder of the three boys—Bobby Peterson and the Schuessler brothers, John and Anton.

Judge Recognizes Irish Republic

In 1920, a native of Ireland appeared before Judge Marcus Kavanagh of the Superior Court to request U.S. citizenship. At that time, the Irish were still citizens of Great Britain, though they were enmeshed in a fierce struggle for independence. When it came time for the petitioner to renounce her foreign citizenship, Kavanagh required her to renounce her status not as a citizen of Great Britain, but instead as a citizen of the "Irish Republic." Kavanagh, a judge from Chicago, thus gave the newly proclaimed Irish government its first official recognition in a US federal court.

I give you Chicago. It is not London and Harvard. It is not Paris and buttermilk. It is American in every chitling and sparerib. It is alive from snout to tail.

— H.L. Mencken

Reform is here to stay, and Chicago is no place for a gentleman.

— Gambler Jim O'Leary (1911)

Even More Loopy Laws

Chicago recently revoked some antiquated laws, which doubtless once served some dire need in sustaining law and order. As of October 3, 2001, the following laws were expunged:

- The Mayor shall receive one copy of each daily newspaper published in the city.

- No one shall keep or maintain or frequent Opium Smoking Rooms – penalty not less than $5 or more than $100.

- No person shall swim or bathe in the waters of Lake Michigan adjacent to the city, or any part of the harbor, unless clothed in a bathing suit.

- It is unlawful to keep a museum of anatomy or illustrate the genital organs in books, pamphlets, circulars, pictures, diagrams, models, casts, or other articles.

- No one shall play a musical instrument in any park, playground, bathing beach, public bath, or airport or carry and display any flag or conduct any military parade without a permit.

With the removal of these laws, one may presumably swim nude at Oak Street beach, diagram the genital organs, keep opium dens, and anatomy museums, and conduct military parades in playgrounds, beaches, airports, and public baths at one's leisure.

Labor Unions, Anarchists, Non-Violence, and Dynamite

Chicago prospered after the Great Fire of 1871, but the wealth belonged to a privileged few, such as Phillip Danforth Armour, Marshall Field, Cyrus McCormick, and George Pullman. These men faced constant unrest from their workers, who vied for shorter workdays and better wages and job conditions. In many factories, especially in the slaughterhouses, laborers worked 10 to 12 hour days, six days a week, for little pay.

The nascent labor movement rightly saw that the value of labor was declining with urbanization and the rise of industrial capitalism, with its trajectory toward larger workplaces, more use of technology, and the breakdown of the manufacturing process into small, isolated tasks that required little skill and training. The individual worker was becoming a cheap, easily replaceable cog.

In many factories, laborers worked 10 to 12 hour days, six days a week, for little pay.

At the end of the Civil War, trade unions started organizing to protect workers' rights. They faced considerable resistance from the middle class, including most politicians, economic leaders, and journalists, who often lumped together union leaders, immigrants, communists, and tramps as threats to the common weal.

Within the unions, there was a great diversity of ideology. Some people said they'd be content with an eight-hour workday. Others, including the socialists, communists, and anarchists, wanted revolution. There was considerable overlap among these groups. Albert Parsons and August Spies—both anarchists—were the editors of Chicago's major socialist newspapers and two of the most prominent spokesmen for the socialist movement.

Despite overlaps, Chicago radicals were internally divided. The anarchists had philosophical objections to institutionalized government and centralized directives, which complicated any quest for group unity. One of their thorniest disagreements concerned the question of whether they should ally themselves with organized labor for causes like the eight-hour workday. Parsons and Spies urged the anarchists to cooperate with the unions for practical reasons, in the hope that the unions would help the radicals overthrow the existing order. The alliance between anarchists and trade unions was known as "the Chicago idea."

The radicals were also torn over issues such as when violence is justified, if ever. Parsons and Spies had often called for non-violence at labor rallies. Like the other six anarchists who stood trial for the Haymarket bombing, they maintained that they believed in violence only in self-defense against "force-propped authority," which included the government and capitalist owners. Nonetheless, anarchist rhetoric often invoked dynamite almost mystically, and many anarchists were fascinated with dynamite, which was inexpensive, relatively accessible, and allowed one to carry an intensely destructive weapon in one's coat pocket. In the trial following the renowned Haymarket riot, the prosecution used the anarchists' reverence for dynamite as key evidence to convict the defendants of murder, even when there was no evidence directly linking the defendants to the bomb that went off at the Haymarket event.

May 1 Walkout

International Workers' Day, May 1, is celebrated in every nation except the U.S., Canada, and South Africa. The holiday traces its roots to an event in the U.S.—a one-day nationwide labor strike on May 1, 1886. This event acquired a different meaning in retrospect—it was one of the events leading up to Chicago's Haymarket tragedy on May 4, 1886.

The short-term goal of the May 1 walkout was an eight-hour workday. Many laborers worked 10 to 12 hour days, six days a week, for little pay. The demonstration was a huge success for the labor movement. Hundreds of thousands of laborers across the U.S. joined in the strike on May 1, 1886. Tens of thousands of Chicago workers set aside their tools and joined many demonstrations in the city, including a parade down Michigan Avenue. One of the leaders of this parade was Albert Parsons, the most

The demonstration was a huge success for the labor movement.

prominent English-speaking spokesman in Chicago for the socialist movement, which was dominated by German immigrants. In 1884, Parsons had become the editor of *The Alarm*, Chicago's leading English-language socialist newspaper. That same year, German-born August Spies had assumed leadership of the *Arbeiter-Zeitung*, the German-language counterpart to *The Alarm*. Both newspapers were produced on the top floors of the *Arbeiter-Zeitung* building at 107 Fifth Avenue (now Wells Street).

Parsons and Spies played a leadership role in the nonviolent May 1 demonstrations, but the *Chicago Mail* singled them out as marked men. "Mark them for today," read an editorial in the *Mail* on May 1. "Hold them responsible for any trouble that occurs. Make an example of them if trouble does occur."

Chicago: It's still a frontier town.

— Norman Mark, *Mayors, Madams and Madmen*, 1979

Haymarket: The United States' First Red Scare

On Monday, May 3, 1886, August Spies, editor of the *Arbeiter-Zeitung* socialist newspaper, spoke at a rally for the Lumber Shovers' Union. This gathering took place near McCormick Reaper Works, where union employees who had been locked out were heckling the non-union workers who had replaced them. Spies called for restraint, but a riot broke out. The police showed up with clubs and guns and killed two workers. That night, George Engel, Adolph Fischer, and some other militant anarchists, met in Greif's Hall on Lake Street and scheduled an outdoor protest to take place the next evening at Haymarket on Randolph Street, where farmers came to sell produce.

Spies had not attended the Greif's Hall meeting, but he had been invited to speak at the Haymarket rally. He arrived a little after 8 P.M. to find that the other speakers hadn't shown up, and the crowd of less than 3,000 was dispersing. Spies sent a colleague, Balthasar Rau, to the *Arbeiter-Zeitung* building to see if he could round up a few more speakers. At the *Arbeiter-Zeitung* building, Rau recruited Albert Parsons and Samuel Fielden to speak at the event. Meanwhile, Spies turned a wagon into a makeshift podium and addressed the crowd.

Chicago was on edge after the May 1 demonstrations and the McCormick riot. Local authorities were concerned about the Haymarket event. Mayor Carter Harrison showed up and repeatedly relit his cigar to make sure everyone assembled knew he was watching. He later testified in court that the event was relatively low-key.

The Haymarket rally had dwindled down to a few hundred people by 10:30 P.M., when Inspector John Bonfield arrived with a special force of 175 officers. Captain William Ward ordered those assembled to disperse "immediately and peaceably ... In the name of the people of the state of Illinois." Fielden, who was just finishing his speech, looked up and said, 'Why, Captain, this is a peaceable meeting." When Ward repeated the command, Fielden said, "All right, we will go," and stepped down from the wagon.

At that moment, eyewitnesses reported seeing a "hissing fiend," a ball with a sparkling fuse, fly through the sky. It landed among the police near the wagon. Shrapnel from the bomb tore through the left leg of Officer Matthias J. Degan, killing him instantly.

Terrified, the other officers opened fire on the crowd, shooting some of their own ranks. Seven officers and at least four workers died. Sixty policemen and an unknown number of civilians were injured. Several policemen had limbs amputated and one lost part of his jaw.

> At that moment eyewitnesses reported seeing a "hissing fiend" fly through the sky.

Mayor Harrison pleaded with the police for calm, but Police Inspectors John Bonfield and Michael Schaak launched a reign of terror over Chicago's working-class population. They entered homes without warrants, and arrested, beat, and interrogated hundreds of suspects. The terrified public actively encouraged the witchhunt, and State Attorney Julius Grinnell supposedly ordered, "Make the raids first and look up the law afterward!"

Eight anarchists—August Spies, Albert Parsons, Samuel Fielden, Michael Schwab, Adolph Fischer, George Engel, Louis Lingg, and Oscar Neebe—were tried for the murder of Matthias Degan, the officer who had died in the explosion of the bomb at Haymarket. Though seven officers had died, the defendants were only charged with one murder. Some of the other officers had been slain by bullets when the police fired into their own ranks.

Given the public mood, it would have been almost impossible to find jurors who hadn't already reached a verdict. But the bailiff responsible for providing potential jurors deliberately stacked the panels with people biased against the anarchist defendants. In selecting jurors, the state eliminated all workers, so the jury consisted mostly of middle-class citizens born in the U.S.

> *The jury consisted mostly of middle-class citizens born in the U.S.*

As a result, the trial was something of a show—a courtroom drama with the verdict scripted in advance. The prosecution, the defense, the jurors, the judge, and the defendants all understood this. In the state's version of the story, the defendants were members of a criminal organization of foreigners who had plotted both riot and murder. State Attorney Julius Grinnell overtly pointed to the eight defendants as representatives of a much deeper malignancy. The larger purpose of the trial was to prove that the state could protect society against those who threatened to undermine it. Grinnell insisted on trying the eight anarchists together, which made them seem like co-conspirators, even though several of them had only met for the first time in jail. Judge Joseph Gary overruled defense motions for separate trials.

The defense, led by Captain William P. Black, portrayed the accused as scapegoats who viewed the fatal bomb as the result of an exploitative economic system and saw the trial as a staged cover-up—an effort to hide the flaws of a repressive regime.

The state brought forth an arsenal of theatrical props such as anarchist flags, bloodstained police uniforms, and bomb-making equipment. The defense protested that the defendants were only charged with the murder of one officer, Degan, and the state was presenting evidence that had nothing to do with this crime. Judge Gary overruled them. He allowed the prosecution to invoke the slayings of the other officers, as if they were part of the case.

While the court was in session, Judge Gary often chatted privately with attractive, well-dressed women, whom he allowed to sit beside him during the trial.

The accused, especially Parsons and Spies, knew that their trial was a show, but they welcomed the national spotlight, and they took advantage of it as best they could. The defendants were, in fact, convicted of murder, even though there was no evidence directly linking them to the bomb that killed Officer Degan.

Neebe was sentenced to 15 years. The other seven were sentenced to death. On November 11, 1887, Parsons, Spies, Fischer, and Engel were hanged at the Criminal Courts Building on Hubbard Street. Fielden and Schwab had their sentences commuted to life imprisonment. Lingg killed himself in prison four days before his execution.

Who actually threw the bomb into the Haymarket rally? This remains unsolved. The state never provided evidence directly linking any of the defendants to the bombing. The prosecution named Rudolph Schnaubelt, the brother-in-law of defendant Michael Schwab, as the bomb-thrower, but this charge was based on little evidence, and Schnaubelt was never tried in court. While rounding up suspects, the police had detained Schnaubelt then released him. He was never seen again.

Some clues to the bombing were never investigated, because Judge Joseph Gary overruled them. Among these leads, the most intriguing was the testimony of Indianapolis saloonkeeper John DeLuse. The barkeep claimed on the morning before the bombing, a mustachioed man in a dark suit entered his tavern toting a small bag. The stranger asked the DeLuse about the labor movement. He told the barkeeper that he was traveling from New York to Chicago and said, "[Y]ou will hear of some trouble there very soon." He pointed to the small bag in his hand: "I have got something in here that will work, you will hear of it." Judge Gary overruled the defense's request to hear DeLuse's testimony.

In 1893, the newly elected Democratic governor of Illinois, John Peter Altgeld, reviewed the Haymarket case. On June 26, 1893, he announced that he had found so many errors in the trial that it was "clearly [his] duty" to "grant an absolute pardon to Samuel Fielden, Oscar Neebe, and Michael Schwab."

August Spies, Albert Parsons, Adolph Fischer, George Engel, the four men executed in the wake of the Haymarket trial, are buried at Waldheim Cemetery in Forest Park. Sculptor Albert Weinert designed their monument. The sculpture, a hooded justice crowning a fallen worker with a laurel wreath, was dedicated on June 25, 1893.

The First Police Statue

As a tribute to the officers who died in the Haymarket tragedy, a nine-foot statue of a policeman was erected in Haymarket Square. Dedicated on May 4, 1889, it was the nation's first monument to a police officer. The police were considered the martyrs of the Haymarket riot for many years, but this view shifted with the rise of large labor unions. The monument itself has had a strange history, with numerous moves and defacements. It now stands in the courtyard of the Police Academy at 1300 West Jackson Boulevard.

Murder in the Restroom

Ioan Culianu, a professor in the history of religion at University of Chicago's Divinity School, was slain in an execution-style in the restroom in 1991. The murder terrified both faculty and students—just exactly who was the killer? Could it be a rival scholar vying for Culianu's position? Or perhaps a student who had received a fail on an exam paper?

Though the case remains unsolved, Ted Anton argues in his book—*Eros, Magic, and the Murder of Professor Culianu*—that this homicide was in fact an assassination and was the result of a political conspiracy.

It was revealed that Culianu, a scholar of magic and the occult, had been taunting a far-right coalition in his native Romania. He believed he was safe on American soil, but he was wrong.

The 1968 Democratic National Convention

Prior to the 1968 Democratic National Convention, activists had advocated nonviolent demonstrations. But things got out of hand when Chicago police beat and teargassed protesters for violating a curfew that denied access to city parks after 11 P.M. Nightly confrontations continued from August 24 through August 28. Eight activists were later charged with violation of the 1968 Anti-Riot Act, which made it a federal crime to cross state lines for the purpose of inciting a riot. Tom Hayden was apprehended on August 26, after letting the air out of police car tires. On August 27, Black Panther Bobby Seale gave a speech in Lincoln Park urging demonstrators to meet police violence with violence. On August 28, Abbie Hoffman was arrested and charged with public indecency for having the word "F**K" written on his forehead. (He claimed he was trying to keep the press from taking his photo.) Rennie Davis was taken to the hospital after police clubbed him unconscious. As cops searched the hospital to arrest Davis, activists covered him with a sheet and wheeled him from room to room. Undercover officers reported that Rennie Davis, Jerry Rubin, and Abbie Hoffman urged activists to "Fight the pigs!" Another undercover officer alleged that John Froines and Lee Weiner had sent him to get materials to make Molotov cocktails.

Following the Democratic National Convention, Attorney General Ramsey Clark and the Justice Department were reluctant to prosecute the protesters. Clark saw the confrontations in Chicago as a police riot and was more interested in charging police officers with brutality. But Mayor Richard Daley persuaded his friend, federal judge William Campbell, to summon a grand jury which indicted eight demonstrators—Rennie Davis, David Dellinger, John Froines, Tom Hayden, Abbie Hoffman, Jerry Rubin, Bobby Seale, and Lee Weiner—for violating the Anti-Riot Act. The jury also indicted eight police officers. The jury returned with its indictments on March 20, 1969. By this time, the Nixon administration had taken over, and the new attorney general, John Mitchell, gave the go-ahead to prosecute the protesters.

The Chicago Seven Trial

On September 24, 1969, eight protesters from the 1968 Democratic National Convention faced charges for conspiracy and violation of the Anti-Riot Act. The defendants included Rennie Davis, David Dellinger, John Froines, Tom Hayden, Abbie Hoffman, Jerry Rubin, Bobby Seale, and Lee Weiner first known as the "Chicago Eight" and later as the "Chicago Seven."

Yippies Hoffman and Rubin turned the trial into a publicity stunt.

The trial was stacked against the defendants from the start, because Judge Julius Hoffman refused to permit inquiry into the cultural biases of any of the potential jurors. The jury consisted of eight white women, two black women, and two white men. The jurors were severely biased against the defendants—one juror said after the trial that the defendants "should be convicted for their appearance, their language, and their lifestyle." Another juror said they "should have been shot down by the police."

The defendants approached the trial with vastly different strategies. While Hayden wanted to observe courtroom decorum and focus on winning the trial by exposing weaknesses in the state's case, Yippies Hoffman and Rubin turned the trial into a publicity stunt. For instance, they wore judicial robes, blew kisses to the jury, bared their chests, and placed a National Liberation Front flag on the defense table. Black Panther Bobby Seale insisted on his right to represent himself or postpone the trial until his own attorney could represent him. Seale also hurled bitter epithets at Judge Hoffman, calling him "racist," "pig," and "fascist dog." The judge had Seale bound and gagged on October 29. On November 5, he sentenced Seale to four years in prison for contempt of court and gave him a separate trial. The Chicago Eight became the Chicago Seven.

District Attorney Thomas Foran and his young assistant, Richard Schultz, built their case around the testimony of three undercover officers, Irwin Bock, William Frappolly, and Robert Pierson, who described "hit-and-run guerilla tactics," including plots to stop traffic and "sabotage" restrooms. J. Anthony Lukas, who witnessed the trial and recounted the event in *The Barnyard Epithet and Other Obscenities*, wrote that, "Schultz could have made the first robin of spring look like a plot by the Audobon Society."

Defense attorneys William Kunstler and Leonard Weinglass depicted the defendants as idealists who responded spontaneously to police violence. They argued that the alleged conspirators had never met as a group and their so-called conspiracy—including Yippie plans to lace Chicago's water supply with LSD—was strictly play. Defense witness Norman Mailer testified that the defendants were "incapable of conspiracy because they're all egomaniacs." Hoffman said, "Conspiracy? Hell, we couldn't agree on lunch."

> Hoffman said, "Conspiracy? Hell, we couldn't agree on lunch."

As soon as the jury began deliberations, Judge Hoffman sentenced the defendants and their two defense attorneys to prison on 159 contempt specifications. The jury acquitted all defendants of the conspiracy charge but found the five defendants guilty of crossing state lines in order to incite a riot.

On November 21, 1972, the Seventh Circuit Court of Appeals reversed all convictions on the grounds that Judge Hoffman refused to permit inquiry into the cultural biases of potential jurors and displayed a "deprecatory and often antagonistic attitude toward the defense." The court also determined that the FBI had wired the defense attorneys' offices with the complicity of the judge and prosecutors.

Great One-Liners from the Chicago Seven

On February 20, 1970, Judge Hoffman sentenced Chicago Seven members Rennie

Davis, David Dellinger, Tom Hayden, Abbie Hoffman, and Jerry Rubin. Each of the activists made a statement before sentencing.

Rennie Davis declared his intentions to "move next door to [prosecutor] Tom Foran and bring his sons and daughter into the revolution," as soon as he got out of prison. David Dellinger called the judge "a man who had too much power over too many people for too many years," but added that he admired Hoffman's "spunk." Tom Hayden said, "We would hardly have been notorious characters if they left us alone on the streets of Chicago," but due to the police violence, arrests, and trial "we became the architects, the masterminds, and the geniuses of a conspiracy to overthrow the government—we were invented." Since Judge Hoffman was about to leave for vacation in Florida, Abbie Hoffman encouraged him to try LSD: "I know a good dealer in Florida; I could fix you up." Jerry Rubin gave the judge a signed copy of his new book, *Do It!* "Julius," wrote Rubin, "you radicalized more young people than we ever could. You're the country's top Yippie." The judge sentenced each defendant to five years in prison and a $5,000 fine.

The Murder That Sparked the Civil Rights Movement

Emmett Till grew up in South Side Chicago. On August 20, 1955, the 14-year-old Till and his cousin Curtis Jones took a train to the Mississippi Delta to visit family. Emmett's mother, a teacher named Mamie Till Bradley, warned him that the South was much different from Chicago, and black people had to be more cautious in their behavior around whites. Since 1882, more than 500 blacks had been lynched in Mississippi. The Supreme Court's 1954 decision to end segregation in schools in Brown v. Board of Education had only increased racial tensions.

Till and Jones arrived at the home of Till's great-uncle, Mose Wright, on the outskirts of Money, Mississippi on August 21. On August 24, they drove Wright's car into Money and stopped at Bryant's Grocery store. Till ran into some local boys outside of the store and showed them photos of his white friends in Chicago.

One of the boys said, "Hey, there's a [white] girl in that store there. I bet you won't go in there and talk to her." Till entered the store and bought some candy. Reports vary on what happened next. Till either whistled at the store clerk, Carolyn Bryant, or said, "Bye, baby."

Till and Jones quickly forgot the event and didn't tell Mose Wright what had happened. But four days later, early Sunday morning, Carolyn's husband, Roy Bryant, and his half-brother, J. W. Milam, knocked on Wright's door and asked whether three boys were staying with him. Wright led them to Till's bedroom. The men told him to get dressed. Wright begged them to whip Till and let him go, but they left with Till—warning Wright that they would kill him if he told anyone.

Within hours, Mamie Till got word that her son had been kidnapped. She notified Chicago newspapers. Wright reported Bryant and Milam to the sheriff, who arrested the two men.

Till's body was found in the Tallahatchie River with a 75-pound cotton gin fan tied to his neck with barbed wire. His face was so disfigured that Wright could only identify the body by the initialed ring on Till's finger.

Mamie Till had a hard time getting her son's body shipped to Chicago. When it arrived, she identified the body and demanded an open-casket funeral, so that "all the world [could] see what they did to my son." Till had been shot in the side of his head. His nose was broken, his skull smashed, and one eye was gouged out. Fifty thousand people showed up. *Jet Magazine* published photos of Till's body. The *Cleveland Call* and *Post* polled black radio preachers nationwide. Five out of six were preaching about Emmett Till. Half of them insisted that "something be done in Mississippi now." The NAACP called the murder a lynching.

But five prominent attorneys came forth to defend Bryant and Milam. The two men stood trial in a segregated courthouse in Sumner, Mississippi. The state could hardly find any witnesses to testify against the defendants. In 1955 Mississippi, blacks did not accuse whites of crimes without consequences. Finally 64-year-old Mose Wright stepped forth and pointed out Bryant and Milam as the two men who kidnapped his nephew at gunpoint in the wee hours of the morning.

Willie Reed took the stand and testified in a whisper. He had seen Till with Milam, Bryant, and a third man. He had heard screams coming from Milam's barn. Milam had exited the barn with a .45 and asked Reed if he saw anything. Reed had said no. Mamie Till testified that the mangled body was her son. The NAACP rushed the witnesses out of state after their testimony. Neither of the defendants took the stand. On September 23, 1955, the all-white jury found them not guilty. "I feel the state failed to prove the identity of the body," the jury foreman later explained.

A few months later, Bryant and Milam agreed to tell their story to *Look Magazine* for $4,000. The publication ran their confession on January 24, 1956. They claimed they took Till into Milam's barn, beat him with a .45, and stuffed him in a truck. Then they drove him to the Tallahatchie River where they forced him to undress and fired a bullet in his head. They twisted wire around his neck and tied it to a gin fan so the body would sink to the bottom of the Tallahatchie. Then they burned his clothing and shoes.

Bryant and Milam were never legally punished for their crimes, though there was minor punishment of a sort when the local black population drove them out of business by boycotting their store. But the murder convinced black people across the United States that what happened in Mississippi affected them all. It was 100 days after Till's murder that Rosa Parks refused to sit at the back of the bus.

The controversy surrounding this case still continues to this day. The case was reopened by the justice department in 2004. In May 2005, an argument brewed over whether or not to exhume the body of Emmett Till in order to establish his real identity, once and for all. Bertha Thomas, president of the Emmett Till foundation, said that the majority of the family wanted to see the case closed and so opposed the exhumation. However, some of his relatives welcomed the move, saying it would establish whether the body was indeed that of Emmett Till, thereby destroying the defense's original case. The FBI have decided to go ahead with the autopsy to confirm the cause of death and to search for any other evidence, such as a bullet, and his body was exhumed in June 2005. At press time the case was still ongoing.

PART III:
Urban Myths

If we've got a lemon, I don't want to make lemonade. I'd rather just throw out the lemon.

– Mayor of Chicago Jane Byrne, 1979–1983

You know the story. Your neighbor says she heard it from her best friend's brother's aunt who swears she knows a guy who put his toy poodle in the microwave to dry. Only her mom heard it wasn't a poodle. It was a pet iguana or a squirrel.

Urban legends seem to spring from nowhere, arising spontaneously. These tall tales, spread by word-of-mouth, are as contagious as the common cold. You hear the story from your co-workers, then it shows up in your email inbox, and no one knows who unleashed it. It has no author. The teller heard it from someone else who "swears it's true."

Chicagoans love this type of modern-day folklore and, considering the city's history, it's no wonder. The city itself is something like an urban myth that sprouted on the prairie, spread fast and soon grew much bigger than anyone ever dreamed it would be.

Jan Harold Brunvand, who first coined the term "urban legend" in his book *The Vanishing Hitchhiker* (1981), gives several samples from the Windy City. In one, a cab driver picks up a nun in downtown Chicago in December 1941. On the way to her convent, they discuss Pearl Harbor. "It will be over in four years," she says. The driver pulls up to her address and turns to collect his fare, but no one is there. He knocks on the convent door. As he describes the nun to the Mother Superior, he notices a portrait on the wall. "That's her," he says. The Mother Superior smiles and replies, "She's been dead for ten years." The story varies. In another version, a couple picks up a hitchhiker, while traveling to Chicago's 1933 Century of Progress Exposition. As in the nun story, the passenger vanishes in the backseat, and the people

> A man answers the door, hears their story, and says, "That's my wife who died four years ago."

knock at the address she gave them. A man answers the door, hears their story, and says, "That's my wife who died four years ago."

One of Chicago's best-known urban legends is the fiction that Catherine O'Leary and her cow sparked the Great Fire of 1871. O'Leary and her bovine friend were officially absolved in 1997. But the tale remains ingrained in the city's collective unconscious, reminding us that Chicago is built on myth, a city of storytellers and dreamers.

Some myths may surprise you. Savvy Chicagoans claim that *New York Sun* editor Charles Dana named Chicago the "Windy City" in 1893—based on its longwinded politicians, not its blustery weather. But the name "Windy City" appears in newspapers as early as 1876.

> *But "Windy City" appears in newspapers as early as 1876.*

We present the following tales for your amusement. We've debunked some of them and left others for you to decide. Some cannot be proven true or false. Those who believe in ghosts will not be surprised to hear of Oprah's Harpo studio, the apparition of Clarence Darrow, or of Adlai Stevenson's haunted clothes. Others will dismiss such reports. But many Chicagoans are more superstitious than they'd like to admit. Just try telling a Cubs fan that billy goats aren't allowed in Wrigley Field.

Sole Trouble

Adlai Ewing Stevenson II served as Illinois' governor and twice ran against Eisenhower as the Democratic Party's presidential candidate in 1952 and 1956. Later, Stevenson became President John F. Kennedy's ambassador to the United

Nations. In 1965, the great orator of the prairie dropped dead on a street in London. As his family was settling the details of his estate, all his clothing was sent to Chicago's Newberry Library, where it hung on racks in the fifth floor stacks. The ambassador's suits, shirts, socks, trousers, hats, topcoats, ties, sweaters, and shoes remained there for some time. Library employees claimed that after Stevenson's clothing arrived, they felt an eerie presence on the fifth floor. Even library patrons who didn't know about the dead man's clothes reported an odd clamminess pervading the book stacks. Some employees refused to enter the fifth floor, especially at night.

CIA Intrigue at Chicago's Museum of Surgery?

The Museum of Surgery stands on some of Chicago's finest real estate, the 1500 block of North Lake Shore Drive. Few Chicagoans have ever visited this low-rise granite palace that displays the grisly instruments of early surgical procedures. It seems remarkable that the city's most underexposed museum could survive in this lakefront landscape, where co-op prices exceed any other property in town.

The museum's next-door neighbor for the last 45 years has been the Consulate General of Poland, a reputed site of CIA intrigue. Aside from the Soviet Embassy in Washington D.C., no other diplomatic post was more essential to clandestine operations during the Cold War. The Polish Consulate in Chicago topped the list of important "listening posts" in a world of espionage, double agents, and cryptic communications. Since the Museum of Surgery stands next door to the Polish Consulate, many Chicagoans suspect that the CIA made secret use of its antiquated surgical devices. Visits to the museum are by appointment only.

Haunted Harpo Studios

Harpo Studios, just west of the loop on Chicago's West Washington Boulevard, houses the headquarters of global celebrity, billionaire talk show host, and media mogul Oprah Winfrey. But no one in Oprah's production company will work in the building alone or at night. A steady stream of strange occurrences have made Harpo Studio employees squeamish in the after hours. The roots of their fear go back 90 years to July 24, 1915, when the Lake Michigan Cruise steamer, the SS *Eastland*, capsized in the Chicago River—creating the worst inland maritime disaster in American history.

> But no one in Oprah's production company will work in the building alone or at night.

The final death count stands at 844. Most of the victims worked for Western Electric and came from the same neighborhood, the Bohemian enclave of Pilsen. In the immediate aftermath, bodies retrieved from the river and from inside the ship's hull were taken to a dockside building on the north bank of the river. But as the death toll grew, this facility proved too small to accommodate the victims. So city officials sent the dead to the city's old 2nd Regiment Armory on West Washington Boulevard, the same building that houses Oprah's Harpo Studios today. For days, families searched among the corpses, trying to identify their loved ones.

Until recently, few Chicagoans knew that Harpo Studios was the site of this maritime tragedy. But when Oprah transformed the old armory into her production company, her employees knew something was awry. They heard sobs and weeping and felt cold spots and chilly drafts. Eventually they learned that their workplace had served as the city morgue after the *Eastland* disaster. Oprah is apparently sympathetic to her employees' fears and allows them to avoid certain areas of the building, especially after hours.

> Oprah is apparently sympathetic to her employees' fears and allows them to avoid certain areas of the building.

Ghost Lover

Richard T. Crowe has a passion for Chicago's dead, especially those who won't rest in peace. A self-described "literary ghost-hunter," Crowe has tracked the paranormal since his high school days. He believes Chicago's textured past and large immigrant populations have made the city especially hospitable to specters. Since 1979, he has conducted bus tours around Chicago focusing on haunted alleys, theaters, churches, and cemeteries—even including a haunted Hooter's bar.

The Undead Darrow

Clarence Darrow (1857–1938) moved to Chicago in 1888. According to some reports, he never left. A figure bearing a striking likeness to Darrow has been seen pacing the back steps of the Museum of Science and Industry. The specter, dressed in the lawyer's trademark rumpled suit, Borsalino hat, and overcoat, stares across the water then disappears.

No one knows why he haunts the Museum of Science and Industry. Some speculate that Darrow, who championed the teaching of evolution in the Scopes trial, still prefers science to whatever the afterlife has to offer.

Myth of the First Settlers

Jean-Baptiste Point de Sable, who settled on the banks of the Chicago River in the 1780s, is widely recognized as Chicago's founder. But contrary to popular belief, Point de Sable was not the first non-native settler. French explorers found the area in 1673, and by 1700, the French had built a trading post and a mission near the center of present-day Chicago. These early settlers are often overlooked because they left few written records, and because Americans tend to trace their heritage to the British colonies on the East Coast and forget that the French were colonizing North America, especially the Great Lakes region, at the same time.

> These early settlers are often overlooked because they left few written records.

In 1673, French explorers Louis Jolliet and Father Marquette set out along the Fox-Wisconsin portage (near the future site of De Pere, Wisconsin) to explore the Mississippi.

In September, they returned by taking a canoe trip down the Chicago River and thus discovered the future site of Chicago. Jolliet's report to the French government included a description of how the Chicago portage linked the Mississippi to the Great Lakes.

Within 30 years, traders had set up posts in what is now Chicago. Via the Green Bay Indian Trail, they traveled overland between Chicago and another settlement at De Pere, Wisconsin.

Today, one can still follow the path of the Green Bay Indian Trail by walking along Clark Street. This street runs along a beach ridge of ancient Lake Chicago. At Foster Avenue, it veers northwest to Howard Street. In Evanston, it turns into Chicago Avenue, then becomes Green Bay Road in the northern suburbs.

A Questionable Name and a Foul Smell

New York, Los Angeles, and San Francisco all have relatively easy names, compared to Chicago. The first recorded use of *Checagou* occurs in the 1680 writings of French explorer René Robert Caviler, Sieur de la Salle. Most historians believe that La Salle reached Chicago in 1679—after Louis Jolliet and Father Marquette who were the first Europeans to visit the site in 1673. Following La Salle's report, the French cartographer Jean-Baptiste Louis Franquelin depicted the two branches of the Chicago River on his 1684 map of the Great Lakes region. He

> *This piquant, eye-watering odor saturated the neighborhoods, especially on rainy days.*

labeled the mouth of the river *Cheagoumeman* and wrote *R. Checagou* on a small stream running from the lakeshore to the Des Plaines River. On his 1686 map, Amerique Septentrion labels a settlement on the south branch of the Chicago River *Chicagou*.

According to William Barry, the first secretary of the Chicago Historical Society, "Whatever may have been the etymological meaning of the word *Chicago* in its practical use, it probably denoted strong or great. The Indians applied this term to the Mississippi River, to thunder, or to the voice of the great Manitou."

Though Barry's definition still appears on the Chicago Public Library's website, Michael Mccafferty, a linguist at Indiana University, has recently presented research supporting an old urban legend about the city's name. In the language of the Miami and Illinois Indians, *chicagou* means "striped skunk" or "wild leek," a member of the garlic group. The word was later used as an adjective meaning "foul-smelling."

This was an apt name during the heyday of the Chicago Stockyards. From 1865 to 1970, you could smell the influx of hundreds of thousands of cows, pigs, and sheep. This piquant, eye-watering odor saturated the neighborhoods, especially on rainy days when the dank cloud cover put a ceiling cap on the city.

The Fort That Never Was

Father Hennepin, a French Jesuit, traveled with Robert Cavelier, Sieur de la Salle when he explored North America. After returning to France, the priest authored an account of his adventures in the New World. His book, which was published in 1697, included some illustrations and maps, but unfortunately Hennepin's drawing of Fort Miami and the St. Joseph River in Michigan was rendered so poorly that later cartographers mistook it for a drawing of the Chicago area. For the next century and a half, maps of that region included the mysterious French Fort.

In 1795, General "Mad Anthony" Wayne, who had sorely defeated the Native Americans at Fallen Timbers, met with representatives from a number of tribes—the Wyandot, Delaware, Shawnee, Ottawa, Chippewa, Miami, Eel River, Wea, Kickapoo, Piankashaw, Kaskaskia, and Potawatomi, who then lived in Chicago. In the resulting Treaty of Greenville, the tribes ceded parts of Ohio, Indiana, Michigan, and "one piece of land, six miles square at or near the mouth of the Chicago River, emptying into the southwest end of Lake Michigan, where a fort formerly stood."

> For the next century and a half, maps of that region included the mysterious French Fort.

The six-square-mile tract covers a sizable chunk of present-day Chicago, bounded by the lakeshore on the east, Cicero Avenue on the west, Fullerton Avenue on the north, and 31st Avenue on the south. According to legend, this land was not originally part of the treaty but Wayne insisted that the Indians surrender the "French Fort," that was pictured on contemporary maps. The Indians had no idea what Wayne was talking about as the fort probably never existed.

This fort was simply the result of bad cartography, from Hennepin's poor rendition of the area. But Mad Anthony insisted, until the Indians said, "Fine. Take the fort. It's yours." The U.S. thus acquired a fort that never was—but they also claimed part of Chicago.

Local historian John Swenson notes that the fort mentioned in the Treaty of Greenville "may be the same as the Petit Fort or 'Little Fort' of various British and American accounts of 1779–1803, and the mythical progenitor of the later settlement at Waukegan."

Rudolph the Drunken Reindeer

In 1949, "Singing Cowboy" Gene Autry recorded the song "Rudolph the Red Nosed Reindeer," which sold an unprecedented two million copies its first year alone and became the second best-selling song of all time (the first is still "White Christmas").

According to urban myth, the song is actually about a holiday drinker—the brainchild of a Montgomery Ward employee in Chicago. The myth is half true. The credit for the underdog reindeer goes to Robert L. May, a copy editor at Montgomery Ward's Chicago headquarters. In 1939, the department store was scouting for a catchy Christmas gimmick. May wrote some rhyming couplets about a sad-sack reindeer whose nose lit up like a light bulb. He tested the verse on his four-year-old daughter. When she gave her approval, May and illustrator, Denver Gillen, visited Chicago's Lincoln Park Zoo to sketch real-life reindeer and created a booklet to present to their bosses.

At first, Montgomery Ward executives did worry that the reindeer Rudolph's red nose might be seen as a parody of the proverbial holiday drunk. May went to great lengths to ensure that his reindeer would not project the image of an inebriate.

The result was a huge marketing success. In 1939, Montgomery Ward distributed 2.4 million copies of May's booklet. World War II paper shortages limited printing, but by 1946, 6 million copies had reached consumers, who flocked to Rudolph's nose (and to Montgomery Ward) like moths to a flame.

Catherine O'Leary and Her Cow Burn Down the City

The autumn of 1871 was unusually dry. Twenty-five fires broke out within three weeks. Any of those blazes could have engulfed the tinderbox city of wooden streets and poorly zoned industrial neighborhoods, haphazardly mixed with residential strips.

On October 7, firefighters transported all of Chicago's fire equipment to the western edge of the city to extinguish a stubborn blaze, which damaged most of the apparatus beyond repair. The fire brigade was dragging its broken equipment back across town on October 8, when the lookout in the City Hall tower spotted plumes of smoke—the first signs of the Great Fire of 1871.

This blaze was worse due to unusual prairie winds that rose up and drove a whirlwind of flames, which roared for three days. A rainfall finally quenched the fire on the evening of October 10, but by this point the conflagration had wiped out three-fifths of the central business district.

Any of those blazes could have engulfed the tinderbox city of wooden streets

In the official police enquiry, no one was singled out as the cause of the Great Fire. But in the ensuing weeks, countless muckracking reporters swept through the city, seeking sensational stories. They latched on to an Irish immigrant, Catherine O'Leary, who lived with her husband Patrick and family in three rooms of a cottage at 558 De Koven Street. At 8:30 P.M. on Sunday October 8, 1871, Catherine allegedly stepped into the shed to milk Daisy, her cow. Supposedly Daisy kicked over a kerosene lamp—sparking a fire that soon engulfed most of Chicago within two hours. Fingers were pointed, accusations hurled. Both Catherine and Patrick O'Leary signed affidavits that no one in their family had entered the shed after nightfall. Some claimed that boys had been smoking in the hayloft. But the O'Learys took the fall. Though their house survived the fire, they left their neighborhood in shame and had to move to a new community on the far south side of town. On October 7, 1997, the Chicago City Council, led by Alderman Edward M. Burke, approved a resolution absolving Catherine O'Leary and her cow of blame for the Great Fire of 1871.

Today the Chicago Fire Department Training Academy stands on the former site of the O'Leary house. Gangster Big Jim O'Leary was actually Catherine O'Leary's son.

Honest Abe

In the pantheon of U.S. presidents, Illinois-born Abraham Lincoln enjoys an almost mythic status. However, people easily forget that he was underappreciated during his lifetime. Though Illinois always loved "Honest Abe," many other Americans viewed him as a bumbling oaf or petty tyrant. Even his own secretary of state, William H. Seward expressed contempt at the beginning of his administration.

But Abe's public image quickly changed following his assassination. He became a martyr for freedom and an icon of humanitarianism. In January 1863, Lincoln signed the Emancipation Proclamation, freeing slaves in confederate states. Today, many Americans see this act as the culmination of Lincoln's lifelong opposition to slavery. But such acts are rarely, if ever, the work of a single individual. The Lincoln administration made the decision, and administrations, like individuals, have complicated agendas. Historians have long puzzled over why Lincoln's hand shook when he signed the Emancipation Proclamation. Was it the weight of national destiny on his shoulders? The physiological effect of too much presidential handshaking? Or did Lincoln fear he was making a mistake—perhaps succumbing to peer pressure?

Lincoln was deeply torn over the decision to free slaves in the confederacy. He said, "In a certain sense the liberation of slaves is the destruction of private property." This is hardly a humanitarian sentiment. Of course, it's hard not to destroy private property when one is at war. From the point of view of military history, the Emancipation Proclamation was almost certainly a strategic decision to weaken the economic base of the confederacy.

So perhaps Abe's motives weren't strictly humanitarian. But was "Honest Abe" honest? It's impossible to answer such questions about someone who died 140 years ago. But consider his rise to presidency. Lincoln had a meager public record when the Republican Party nominated him as their presidential candidate in

1860. He had briefly served as a congressman from Illinois, but he was little known outside the state, and his contender for the Republican nomination was Senator Stephen Douglas, one of Illinois' most successful politicians of the time. But the Republican National Convention of 1860 took place in Chicago, and the city's mayor Long John Wentworth was so devoted to Lincoln that he orchestrated street demonstrations and produced thousands of counterfeit credentials in order to pack the convention hall with Lincoln supporters. Delegates supporting other candidates were turned away at the door. In short, the mayor of Chicago rigged Lincoln's nomination. Honest Abe may have been honest, but those who put him in the White House were anything but.

The Windy City

Chicagoans rarely refer to their home as "the Windy City," but many assume that the nickname derives from the city's skin-piercing, umbrella-bending winter gales. The city sits on the flatland of the prairie at the lower end of Lake Michigan— where blustery winds are common. According to those in the know, the nickname is more political than climatic. When the international committee met to select the site for the 1893 World's Columbian Exhibition, they considered proposals from individual cities. Chicago's advocates made such long-winded arguments on behalf of their city that New York Sun editor Charles Dana dubbed Chicago "the Windy City."

But this may be an urban myth as well. Barry Popik, a New York City parking-ticket judge by day, word sleuth by night, scoured newspapers and magazines of the late nineteenth century, and found that Chicago's nickname switched from the Garden City to the Windy City around 1876. Popik found the following references:

"THAT WINDY CITY. Some of the Freaks of the Last Chicago Tornado" (headline), *Cincinnati Enquirer*, pg. 2, col. 4, May 9, 1876.

"CHICAGO LETTER—Gossip and Impressions of the Windy City" (headline), *Cincinnati Enquirer*, pg. 5, col. 2, Feb. 12, 1877.

Chicago seems a big city instead of merely a large place.

— A.J. Liebling

The Billy Goat Curse

Despite all the ghost stories in this collection, most Chicagoans don't believe in a world of curses and mystical vendettas. Nor do most Cubs fans. But even those who think themselves immune from superstition pale at the thought of the Billy Goat curse.

In 1934, William Sianis purchased the Lincoln Tavern with a check for $205. The check bounced, but Sianis sold enough liquor the first weekend to repay the money. An animal lover, the saloonkeeper happily adopted a goat that wandered into his tavern after tumbling off a passing truck. As people take after their pets, so Sianis grew a goatee. Patrons began calling him "Billy Goat" Sianis, and he even renamed his bar the Billy Goat Tavern, which now goes by the slogan, "Butt in anytime."

Sianis was also a master of the publicity stunt. An example of this is when the Republican National Convention came to Chicago in 1944—he posted a sign in the window that read, "No Republicans allowed." Instead the trick worked and Republicans flooded into the bar, demanding service. This shunted Sianis to stardom in Chicago, a Democratic holdout in the Midwest.

> Sianis loved the Chicago Cubs, who were then one of the nation's most successful baseball teams.

But true fame came to Billy Goat during the 1945 World Series. Sianis loved the Chicago Cubs, who were then one of the nation's most successful baseball teams. From 1876 to 1945, they had a 5475–4324 (.559) record, with 51 winning seasons, 16 first place finishes, and 16 pennants and World Series appearances. They won two World Series titles and six Championship titles. But in game four of the 1945 World Series, their luck turned sour.

On October 6, 1945, the Cubs entered game four of the World Series leading the Detroit Tigers two games to one. To win the World Series, the Cubs needed to win only two of the next four games.

"Billy Goat" Sianis bought two tickets to game four—one for himself and one for his pet goat, Murphy. But ushers stopped the saloonkeeper at the entrance to Wrigley Field, saying no animals allowed. Billy Goat appealed to P. K. Wrigley, owner of the Cubs.

"Let Billy in, but not the goat," said Wrigley.

"Why not the goat?" Billy asked.

"Because the goat stinks."

According to urban myth, Sianis shook his fist at the heavens and exclaimed, "The Cubs ain't gonna win no more. The Cubs will never win a World Series so long as the goat is not allowed in Wrigley Field."

Some say that from that day on, the team's fortune reversed. The Cubs lost game four and the rest of the 1945 World Series. Sianis sent a telegram to P. K. Wrigley, asking, "Who stinks now?"

From 1946 to 2003, the Cubs posted a 4250–4874 (.466) record, had only 15 winning seasons, finished in first place a mere 3 times, and had no pennants. They have not played in a World Series since 1945.

Nephew Tries to Lift Curse

In 1973, the Cubs were enjoying a mid-season first-place lead. *Tribune* columnist Dave Condon arranged for the new owner of the Billy Goat Tavern, Sianis' nephew Sam, to bring a goat to Wrigley Field to lift the curse. Sam Sianis chose a goat named Socrates, who was descended from Murphy, the goat denied entrance in 1945. The goat rode to Wrigley Field in a white limousine, where he received a red carpet welcome with a sign reading, "All is forgiven. Let me lead the Cubs to the pennant." But the ushers turned the goat away again, and the Cubs first-place lead withered into another season of losses.

Tokyo Rose

Many urban myths surround Iva Ikuko Toguri d'Aquino, a Japanese-American woman convicted of treason following World War II. The main myth is that Iva deliberately harassed Allied troops as the voice of "Tokyo Rose" on English-speaking Radio Tokyo.

Iva, born in the U.S. in 1916, sailed to Japan in 1941 to care for an aging aunt. Unfortunately, she left the country without a U.S. passport, and when she tried to return home, immigration officials wouldn't let her back in the country. In Japan, Iva applied for a U.S. passport, but before her application was processed, the Japanese bombed Pearl Harbor and American authorities—who were busy shuttling Japanese Americans to internment camps—ignored her request. Stuck in Japan, Iva was harassed by the Japanese government as an "enemy alien." In 1943, she was forced to work, alongside other English-speaking women, as a broadcaster on Radio Tokyo's "Zero Hour." Under the alias "Orphan Ann," she allegedly taunted the Allied troops in the South Pacific: "Hiya, keeds, I mean all you poor abandoned soldiers, sailors and Marines vacationing on those lovely tropical islands. Gets a little hot now and then, doesn't it? Well, remember, fellas, while you're sweating it out on the islands, your sweet little patootie back home is having a hotcha time with some friendly defense worker. They're probably dancing right now to this number . . . it used to be your song . . . remember?" Then she played a song intended to make the troops homesick.

Iva was the only civilian at Radio Tokyo who refused to renounce her U.S. citizenship. But ironically, when World War II ended, she was high on the list of war criminals. The press dubbed her "Tokyo Rose" —the Allied troops' general name for Japanese female broadcasters. Charged with treason, Iva pleaded innocent. She claimed that she—along with three American POWs—had been forced to taunt the Allied troops, but they had made their broadcasts deliberately ridiculous in order to subvert the Japanese propaganda. She was nonetheless convicted of treason and sent to federal prison.

In 1956, Iva got out of prison early for good behavior. She moved to Chicago, where she worked at the family store until well into her 80s. Few customers knew of her tragic wartime past.

In the 1970s, journalists began to reexamine Iva's case as an example of anti-Japanese racism and hysteria. Two witnesses who had testified against her confessed that the prosecutor had coached them. In 1977, President Gerald R. Ford issued Iva a full and unconditional pardon. It was the first time in U.S. history that a pardon was granted to someone convicted of treason.

Gangland Ghosts

A senior citizens' project now stands in place of the Clark Street garage, but a few trees mark the site of the Saint Valentine's Day slaughter of 1929, when henchmen of Al Capone murdered members of the Moran gang. Some say that dogs recoil from those trees, and nearby residents report crying and moaning late at night.

The Lipstick Killer

In July 1946, 17-year-old William George Hierens confessed to three brutal slayings. Newspapers assured Chicagoans that they could breathe easier now that "the werewolf was in chains." But Bill Hierens, an avowed petty thief, insists that he never committed the murders and only confessed under ruthless interrogation, pressure from his lawyers, and fear of the electric chair.

Chicago witnessed a surge of crime after World War II, partly due to the return of soldiers who were traumatized by combat and could not find gainful employment. Across the nation, the murder rate rose 32 percent since the previous year. In the first ten days of December 1945, Chicago reported 265 burglaries, 109 robberies, 109 stolen autos, 8 murders and 4 rapes. Citizens feared a return to the days of Prohibition and Al Capone. Law enforcement failed to stem the flood of crime. Worst of all, police had no concrete leads in the ruthless ritualistic killings of two women and a six-year-old girl. The press dubbed the unknown slayer "The Lipstick Killer" because he scrawled on a victim's wall in lipstick, "For heavens sake catch me before I kill more. I cannot control myself."

On June 26, 1946, police nabbed Bill Hierens, a 17-year-old University of Chicago student who robbed compulsively and could climb, crawl, and break into buildings with uncanny, Houdini-like skill. Police cornered Hierens on a fire escape during one of his housebreakings and knocked him unconscious with a flowerpot when he drew a gun.

Hierens awoke in the hospital surrounded by police, who hurled accusations and interrogated him day and night. Under the influence of sodium

> "For heavens sake catch me before I kill more. I cannot control myself."

pentothal (truth serum), Bill spoke of an uncontrollable shadowy alter ego, "George," who committed his crimes for him. The press latched onto this and created a sensation—a 17-year-old Dr. Jekyll and Mr. Hyde.

The state had only circumstantial evidence. Many people still believed Hierens was being framed, but the press and his police interrogators had already found him guilty. The state's attorney offered him a plea bargain: confess to three murders and avoid the electric chair. Hierens lawyers advised him to accept. The state assured him that even if he was found innocent of the murders, his burglary convictions would mean life imprisonment.

> The state's attorney offered him a plea bargain: confess to three murders and avoid the electric chair.

As the lawyers hammered out the plea bargain, the newspapers waited anxiously, vying for the year's best scoop. But the *Chicago Tribune* jumped the gun and ran a fictional confession as if it were fact. When Hierens heard the fictional confession on the radio in his cell, he decided to accept the plea bargain. He claims that he invented his own confession based on the *Tribune*'s version and changed the story whenever his lawyers asked, "Now Bill, is that really the way it happened?" Hierens, now 77, is still behind bars, serving three life sentences. Aside from his plea bargain, he has always professed innocence. Some researchers believe him. Others are convinced of his guilt. One thing is certain: Bill Hierens never received a fair trial.

A city in conflict... caught between the wish to be sophisticated and yet remain a pioneer town. It [possessed] some of the virtues of the larger city and some of its vices, some of the virtues of a village and some of its vices.

— *Before I Kill More* by Lucy Freeman

Those Superstitious Baseball Fans

In 2004, the Boston Red Sox won the World Series after almost a century-long drought. The Chicago Cubs now hold the record for World Series-less seasons, and diehard fans will try anything to break the curse. Since musician Jimmy Buffett played at Boston's Fenway Park for the 2004 World Series, Chicago city officials are already negotiating with the Cubs, who must secure local residents' approval to stage a Jimmy Buffett concert at Chicago's Wrigley Field—in the hope that whatever juju Buffett unleashed at Fenway Park will do the trick for Chicago.

Chicago's South Side Drag Queens: From the 1920s through the '50s

Numerous myths surround the history of gays and lesbians in the early to mid 20th century. For instance, it is widely assumed that the 1969 Stonewall riots in New York City launched the gay liberation movement and dramatically increased gay visibility, while before 1969, gays and lesbians kept a low profile—especially during Senator Joseph McCarthy's anti-homosexual witchhunt of the 1950s.

While many gays and lesbians took refuge in the closet during the Cold War era, drag balls were flourishing on Chicago's South Side. The ironically named Finnie's Balls—founded by Alfred Finnie, a black gay hustler—reached their height of popularity and visibility in the '50s.

The balls, held on Halloween and New Year's Eve, took place in predominantly poor black working-class neighborhoods, but they drew spectators from a wide range of ethnic and class backgrounds. Moreover, at a time when white middle-class society was largely opposed to homosexuality, the black press, including the *Chicago Defender*, *Jet* and *Ebony* covered the balls extensively and published captioned photos.

While Finnie launched his drag balls in 1935, his were not the first.

While Finnie launched his drag balls in 1935, his were not the first. It's unclear when Chicago's drag balls began, though newspapers mentioned drag queens attending Hinky Dink Kenna and Bathhouse Coughlin's First Ward Ball in 1907.

Myles Vollmer, a divinity student at the University of Chicago, wrote the following between 1929 and 1933: "Twice a year, with the knowledge and protection of Chicago's officialdom, do the homosexuals of the city gather in great numbers for their semi-annual costume ball, at which conventions and repressions are flung to the winds. New Year's Eve, and Halloween, mark the occasions for the celebrations of the 'shadow world.'"

As remarkable as this description is, Vollmer was wrong about a few things. According to scholar Allen Drexel, gay gatherings and drag performances were not restricted to semi-annual balls or even to private homes. From the 1920s through the '40s, homosexuals of both sexes and various races hung out in jazz and blues clubs on Chicago's South Side. The Cabin Inn at 35th and South State Street featured same-sex and interracial dancing as well as a transvestite chorus line. An "all-female" (cross-dressed) chorus line also danced at Joe's Deluxe, another South Side club, during the '40s.

Public display was risky for drag queens—it violated social conventions and a city ordinance, which prohibited one from wearing "a dress not belonging to his or her sex" in public. Nonetheless, drag queen "Nancy Kelly," born Lorenzo Banyard in 1917, recalls drag queens socializing on South Side streets in the early 1940s: "They'd be comin' down the street corner swishin' all over Michigan Avenue to catch the bus to go to the club, you know. And I'd be standing on the corner of Forty Third Street, 'cause I *admired* them, you know, they had this long hair. . . and the makeup and everything . . . Plus they was making money, too, for dancing."

Along the Waters Edge

Calvary Cemetery in suburban Evanston abuts Chicago's northside and lies so close to Lake Michigan that crashing waves spray the cemetery's entrance during winter storms. The surrounding region, between Northwestern and Loyola University, is filled with college students and has witnessed more than a few drownings. Passing motorists sometimes report a young man, soaking wet, staggering into the cemetery at night. Others say they see a figure emerging from the waters, pleading for help.

Music and Sadness in the Air

Between 1838 and 1848, countless Irish immigrants sought their fortune on the digging gangs that hollowed out the Illinois and Michigan Canal. Many died under wagon wheels, or in canal bed cave-ins, or from infectious diseases that ravaged the laborers. Their remains lie in the nameless graves of St. James at the Sag, one of the oldest Catholic parishes in Chicago.

From the time of the Civil War, visitors have reported hearing music amid the tombstones.

From the time of the Civil War, visitors have reported hearing music amid the tombstones and tumbling prairie winds. Some people have placed the names of ballads and airs from the era of the young homesick canal diggers. Some still claim to hear the tunes despite the surrounding suburban sprawl.

Musical Chairs

One afternoon in 1930, 16-year-old Catherine Ryan returned from school and was struck blind as she walked into the dining room of her Southside Chicago home on 51st Street. As her Irish-born mother ran to her side, the dining room chairs levitated and spun around the table. Young Catherine said she heard a voice pleading with her to have a Mass offered for the previous owner of the house, a Lithuanian man who had died. Ma Ryan summoned her parish priest, the Lithuanian Father Jonelis, who agreed to offer a Mass in the house for the deceased resident. Shortly after the conclusion of the liturgy, Catherine screamed. Her sight had returned completely. The priest forbade the Ryans to speak of the events. But they couldn't keep quiet, and soon everyone knew about the Lithuanian ghost.

Resurrection Mary

Motorists traveling along Archer Avenue near Chicago's southside Resurrection Cemetery report a shapely blond woman who lunges out the shrubbery waving them down for a ride. Drivers have slammed their brakes, only to see the girl run into the cemetery and disappear among the gravestones. Winter or summer, she is said to wear the flouncy gown of a past era. Some believe that she is "Resurrection Mary," a young Polish woman, who died in 1931 in a car crash on her way home from a dance at Willowbrook Ballroom.

Winter or summer, she is said to wear the flouncy gown of a past era.

Last Survivor of the Boston Tea Party

David Kennison achieved notoriety as the "last surviving participant of the Boston Tea Party." His grave lies on the rolling lawn just behind the administration building of the Lincoln Park Zoo. At the site stands a boulder and a plaque, recognizing Kennison as a veteran of one of the nation's most critical encounters with its colonial overseers. David claimed to have been born in 1736 and died at age 116. His claims have been questioned, but never debunked.

Visitors in the Night

In the sanctuary wall of Chicago's Holy Family Church, there is a statue of two boys, dressed in acolyte robes, each genuflecting on one knee. The church's founder, Jesuit Father Arnold Damen, always claimed there was a story behind this statue. One night in the 1880s, two boys in acolyte robes woke him up and said that their mother was dying and needed a priest to administer last sacraments. Damen said the boys guided him with their candle to a small shanty, where he climbed the stairs and found an old Irish woman, alone and near death. She was startled that the well-known priest had shown up, and that he had been able to find her. He told her he found her easily, thanks to the help of her two boys who guided him through the streets. The woman said that her two sons had died years ago in childhood.

Royal Faux Pas

One late member of the House of Windsor enjoys a peculiar place in Chicago's urban myths. Princess Margaret, sister of Queen Elizabeth II, made a rare visit to Chicago in 1979, shortly after IRA extremists assassinated her uncle, Lord Louis Mountbatten in Ireland. Jane Byrne, Chicago's first and only woman mayor, had attended Mountbatten's funeral at Westminster Abbey as part of a U.S. delegation representing President Jimmy Carter. When Byrne heard the princess was coming to town, she invited her to dinner. Princess Margaret was understandably upset over the murder of her uncle. At dinner, she supposedly went on a diatribe in which she declared to Mayor Byrne, "The Irish are pigs."

> At dinner, she supposedly went on a diatribe in which she declared to Mayor Byrne, "The Irish are pigs."

The comment sparked fury, particularly among Chicago's large Irish population. Trying to downplay the situation, Mayor Byrne claimed that the princess had actually said, "The Irish like jigs." No one believed this, and Princess Margaret cancelled her visit to Boston following the Chicago fiasco. But what could she expect? "Chicago don't cotton to royalty," as Mayor Long John Wentworth said more than 150 years ago, during the visit from her great grand uncle, Bertie, the Prince of Wales.

Candy Heiress Thrown to the Dogs

Like Hershey or Heinz, the name Brach enjoys instant recognition—having hitched a ride into millions of American homes on the back of pieces of hard candy. Helen Brach, scion of Chicago's Brach Candy empire, resided in a stately mansion with a household staff responsible for the everyday details of her life. But in February 1977, the candy heiress disappeared. She was last seen leaving the Mayo Clinic in Rochester, Minnesota.

Brach employee John Matlick, told police that he drove his employer to Chicago's O'Hare Airport for a flight to Florida on February 21, 1977. He officially reported her missing on March 3. A mad nationwide search ensued, but no trace of Helen turned up. In May 1984, she was pronounced dead.

Nonetheless, during the search, the police followed a number of leads, and one of them gave birth to an urban legend. Shortly before Helen Brach's disappearance, Matlick had bought an industrial-strength food grinder to prepare meals for Helen's pets, a pair of Great Danes. Many believe that Matlick turned his employer into dog food and fed her to her own canines.

Unwitting Cannibals

Chicago's mob bosses had a practice of grinding their enemies into sausage meat. This is apparently a convenient way to dispose of a corpse and may account for many unsolved murders and odd disappearances—people who were never heard from again and bodies never found. Countless police reports contain testimony that some gangland chief threatened to turn some poor sap in to sausage if he failed to pay his

> Chicago's mob bosses had a practice of grinding their enemies into sausage meat.

mafia-enforced "juice loans." Since many mobsters ran neighborhood restaurants, Chicagoans began to suspect that the tangy spice-filled meat that topped their pizza might contain the last earthly remains of a disloyal thug or an ill-starred witness against organized crime. It's enough to make one think twice before biting into a pizza.

Hitler's Revenge

George Cardinal Mundelein, the Brooklyn-born son of German immigrants, served as Archbishop of Chicago from 1916 to 1939. He drove a red Dussenberg, the German answer to the Rolls Royce, and entertained President Franklin Delano Roosevelt over for lunch at his Chicago house.

In May 1937, Mundelein gained an international spotlight through his outspoken criticism of Hitler. He referred to the German Chancellor as "an Austrian paper-hanger, and a poor one at that." The comment unleashed Hitler's rage, much to the amusement of Roosevelt, who shared a distaste for dictators.

In October 1939, the cardinal was found dead in his country mansion on the campus of his Chicago seminary, some 50-miles from downtown. According to official reports, he died in his sleep of a cerebral hemorrhage. But since he had denounced Hitler, rumors spread that agents of the Third Reich had offed the cardinal in his sleep.

Rats in the Toilet

During the late 1950s and early 1960s, Chicago embarked on an aggressive campaign to construct a freeway system that crisscrossed the city and carried motorists out to the suburban sprawl. Bulldozers plowed over tens of thousands of houses, most in poor areas of the city, to make way for curving concrete motorways like the Dan Ryan Expressway. The destruction of homes displaced thousands of Chicago residents and ten million rats, who escaped the bulldozers' maws and scurried into city sewers in other neighborhoods. According to legend, many Chicagoans came face-to-face with fat Norwegian rats swimming in their toilets. Though such tales have never been verified, it's enough to make one exercise caution when lifting the lid.

Pachyderms Roar Amid the Tombstones

On June 22, 1918, 400 performers and roustabouts from the Hagenback-Wallace Circus were riding by train to Hammond, Indiana for a show the next day. At four A.M., the train stopped to cool an overheated wheel-bearing box. Though the train was flashing its red warning lights, an empty troop train, driven by an engineer who had been fired for sleeping on the job, crashed into it at full speed and plowed through three sleeping cars before grinding to a stop. Fire broke out, and some circus performers who had survived the crash were trapped in the wreckage and burned to death. Eighty-six performers perished.

A few months before the accident, the Showman's League of America had bought a burial plot in Woodlawn Cemetery, located in Chicago's leafy western suburb, Forest Park. On June 27, the survivors gathered at the plot, called "Showmen's Rest," for the burial of those who had once dared death-defying stunts. The dead included the "Great Dierckx Brothers," Arthur Dierckx and Max Nietzborn, and Jennie Ward Todd of "The Flying Wards." Some performers were known only by their nicknames. Their stones read, "Baldy" or "Four Horse Driver." But in most cases, no one knew the victims' names. A few days before the crash, the circus had hired a bunch of roustabouts for a show in Michigan City. Their stones read "Unknown Male," followed by a number.

> Fire broke out, and some circus performers who had survived the crash were trapped in the wreckage and burned to death.

Many years later, five stone elephants were placed at the corners of Showmen's Rest burial plot. Each holds a ball under its foot and lowers its trunk in mourning.

According to urban myth, these statues commemorate pachyderms killed in the train wreck. Some say the elephants lost their lives tugging at the burning wreckage to save trapped circus performers. Nonetheless, some guests at Woodlawn Cemetery swear that they hear elephants trumpeting over the graves.

Bumps in the Night

The 160-year-old Bachelor's Grove Cemetery near southwest suburban Oak Forest has the distinction of being the most haunted graveyard in the United States. In the 1950s, a grotesque maniac with hooks for hands terrified young couples, who ventured into the forested surroundings looking for a place to make out. The resemblance to Freddie Kruger of *Nightmare on Elm Street* is no accident. Some say a ghost cottage pops up along the road leading to the cemetery. Others report a pale blue light that flickers across the headstones or a spectral farmhouse, lit from inside, with a porch-swing on the porch. The graveyard's proximity to a state hospital has also inspired rumors that psychiatric patients occasionally slip out and frolic amid the tombstones.

Dead Boys Don't Wear ...

When the eight-year old son of a prosperous Irish Catholic family died in the 1920s, the boy's mother was so distraught that the family spared no expense in embalming the boy before his entombment in a Southside Catholic cemetery. It is said that the mother spent the remainder of her life changing the clothes on the young boy's body once a year. Presumably he was in a crypt so she didn't have to dig him up.

Bozo's Nightmare

WGN, the Chicago television station owned by the *Chicago Tribune*, syndicated "Bozo the Clown Show" nationwide, but the kids' TV show was produced in Chicago. For 40 years, Bozo's "Big Top" was the number-one children's venue in town. Tickets for Bozo were harder to get than Bulls tickets at the height of Michael Jordan's career. Expecting parents added themselves to the list during pregnancy, so their child would have a chance to see the show at age six or seven.

Among many games, the Bozo Show featured "The Bucket Game," a contest in which kids tossed a ball in a series of pails, each progressively farther away. Chicagoans love to tell the story of one child, who manages to throw the ball into each of the buckets until he misses the final toss. The kid lets Bozo have it—belting out a string of expletives that would make a longshoreman blush. And the clown just stands there, shocked at the stream of filth spurting from the kiddy-contestant's mouth. Presumably, post-production editing could have eliminated the blue material—if such an event ever happened. The tale is a prototypical urban myth, in that no one actually witnessed the incident, but the storyteller always seems to know a friend of a friend who was there. True or false, the story captures something of Chicago's character. Today, the child is probably beating people up at a White Sox game.

Roses in December

Mary Alice Quinn, who died in 1935 at age 14, is something of a local holy figure. Before dying, she told her parents she would help the suffering and "shower roses on the world." Since then, devotees have made pilgrimages to her grave in Holy Sepulchre Cemetery, 6001 West 111th Street. People say the smell of roses in December brings them, and some credit her with miracle cures. Some also smell roses in her bedroom in Calumet City.

PART IV:
Oddballs & Weirdos

Henry James would have been vastly improved as a novelist by a few whiffs from the Chicago stockyards.

– H. L. Mencken, *The Smart Set*

In politics the machine runs you or you run the machine. I run the machine.

– Mayor of Chicago Edward J. Kelly, 1933-1947

From its days as a fur-trading post, Chicago lured a wide variety of human wildlife—tavern fiddlers, fur trappers, pioneers, adventure-seekers, sharp-shooters, saloonkeepers, stage coach robbers, and ditch diggers—eager to escape the rigid confines of New England or make their fortune in the New World. Robber barons amassed empires through meatpacking, merchandising, building railroads and buying up real estate. Immigrants arrived from Germany, Ireland,

Italy, Lithuania, Poland, and other nations. Cultures clashed and combined. The Windy City—as a hub of water, land and now air travel—has always been structurally open to outsiders. Throughout the nineteenth century, the most common trait among Chicagoans was that they came from somewhere else. When the rail lines joined in the city, every oddball in the nation passed through. The World's Columbian Exposition of 1893 drew freaks from around the globe. Despite ethnic tensions, racial rifts, anti-vice crusades, and brutal police crackdowns, outsiders have always come in droves.

Of course, one person's freak is another's beloved eccentric. It's just a matter of interpretation. Chicagoans have honored many oddballs—at least in retrospect. Captain George Wellington Streeter, a latter-day explorer, was sailing his private vessel on Lake Michigan when he ran aground on the Chicago Lakefront, checked out the area and called it home. Part entrepreneur, part pirate, Streeter staked a claim on his sandbar, proclaiming it "the District of Lake Michigan," and charged developers a fee to dump their trash on the beach by his boat. He then rented out the landfill, selling plots to tenants who built shacks on the debris. For 15 years, Streeter held his ground against lawsuits and police attacks. The city finally managed to throw him in jail for selling liquor on Sundays, but the land he lorded over is still called "Streeterville."

Chicago has also known real pirates, the swashbuckling Dick Dooley and "One Night Stand" Cullen, ruthless robber barons like streetcar mogul Charles

Yerkes and meatpacking magnate Philip Danforth Armour, who suggested that preachers improve their sermons by including "more of Armour's sausages in their diet" and attributed his success to "keeping [his] mouth shut." In 1899, Chicago real estate grandee Hetty Green was the richest person in the United States—and the most miserly. She lived in squalor and haggled Chicago's Great Northern Hotel down to $2 a week for her room. America's first saint, Mother Francis Xavier Cabrini, was also an odd character, who often butted heads with the church hierarchy. When she visited the Archbishop of Chicago, she always sneaked out a back door—leaving him to pay her cab fare.

From the 1950s through the 1970s, Lar "America First" Daly ran for 40 offices from school superintendent to U.S. president—always campaigning in a full-body Uncle Sam suit, complete with red, white, and blue tuxedo, top hat and white goatee. Chicago still celebrates its eccentrics. Diehard Cubs fans fly Ronnie "Woo-Woo" Wickers around the country so he can belt out his train-whistle-like cheer that's so loud you can hear it on TV.

The Exegetical Thief

Andrew "Handy Andy" Lowe, a burglar of the 1860s, eluded the Chicago cops' most elaborate stakeouts. And he took lots of risks. He announced the house he intended to rob in advance, and once inside, he seemed in no hurry to leave. In fact, he spent hours in his victim's library. Selecting works of philosophy and literature from the shelves, "Handy Andy" would annotate the margins of his victim's books—penciling in fine points of exegesis and scholarship. He always left the volumes open so the victim could read his extensive notes. Perhaps some even grudgingly looked forward to his intellectually stimulating visits. Victims claimed he displayed a nuanced grasp of many disciplines. It was as if a band of professors had robbed them.

The Frankenstein Convict

When James Tracy was sentenced to hang in 1882, he donated his body to science. He gave a group of doctors permission to revive him—after he was declared legally dead. With the cooperation of the Cook County states attorney and the warden of Cook County Jail, the doctors transported Tracy's corpse to a laboratory in the jail, where they attempted to resuscitate the convict.

These electric shocks made his heart and even his leg muscles contract.

In a *Frankenstein*-like procedure, the doctors attempted the ressuscitation by attaching primitive electrodes to Tracy's body and administering electricity. These electric shocks made his heart and even his leg muscles contract.

If the doctors had succeeded in reviving Tracy, one has to wonder about the legal implications—would he have to undergo a second execution, according to law? One could imagine a rather tortuous situation in which a convict who received multiple death sentences would be killed multiple times.

None of this became an issue in Cook County. Revival was out of the question, because Tracy's neck had snapped in the hangman's fall. There was only a moment of spine-chilling hope when an electric shock made the cadaver's eyes open.

Camera Shy Criminal

In 1869, photography was still relatively new. Louis Daguerre had only developed the Daguerreotype process in 1837. Matthew Brady and staff had just made history covering the Civil War. Chicago cops were scrupulously photographing every criminal they nabbed.

"Little Dick" Harris outmaneuvered them. It wasn't that they couldn't arrest him, but they couldn't get him to sit for the camera. When they couldn't hypnotize him, they knocked him out with chloroform to take his photo. Another time, they strapped him to a chair and propped his eyelids open with straws. Who'd think that a mugshot would lead to cruel and unusual punishment?

Onion Ring of Fire

On September 29, 2004, Michael Strauss of Chicago sued the hamburger chain White Castle alleging that when he bit into one of their onion rings in 2002, hot grease spurted out and scalded his arm.

His suit states "White Castle has a duty . . . not to sell food to the general public which is too hot for consumption." He is asking for more than $50,000 in medical expenses.

Cooking with Lasers and Inkjet Printers

Chicago's "mad scientist" chef, Homaro Cantu, says, "Gastronomy has to catch up to the evolution in technology." Cantu uses an inkjet printer to print designs on edible paper, which he uses to make his fishless sushi. At his Moto restaurant, Cantu plans to bake with a "class IV" laser (used in welding and surgery) that cooks the center but not the outside of the dish. He will also develop edible tables, chairs, and eating utensils and make food levitate using superconductors and helium.

Computers Helping Computers

In March 2005, a Chicago-based computer training company called OnDeckTech hired a female robot to give online technical support to Mac users. NaturallyMac is available for live chat and answers emails.

Customers seem pleased with the new hire. "I like that I can count on a quick response after midnight and before 7 A.M. when a human being isn't immediately available," says customer Joe Parisi.

OnDeckTech's professional services department is also adapting. Insurance agent Ralph Kastel says, "Robots can be covered. As long as there's an employee-employer relationship so she may be included in payroll, we will have no trouble fulfilling health and dental benefits as they may apply." But will computer repair companies accept BlueShield? AppleCare was not available for comment.

Others expressed concerns that the robot would replace them.

Worker's compensation is a pricklier issue, especially since NaturallyMac works 168 hours a week. "Our initial concern is wage and hour law," says OnDeckTech's attorney, Jerry Holisky. "We've acted responsibly by ensuring she takes at least two 15-minute breaks each day along with an hour for lunch —whatever lunch may be." "I never thought I'd have to use the works of Isaac Asimov as a reference book on payroll taxes," marvels accountant Greg Mermel.

But some employees are less satisfied with their new coworker. "I like the fact she's female, but are tech-savvy females so rare that we've got to manufacture them?" asks customer serviceperson Erika Shaw.

Others expressed concerns that the robot would replace them. "I feel obsolete," says Jay Cihla. "My morale is at an all-time low."

Technical difficulties can be so frustrating and emotionally charged that many customers prefer to talk to another human, but others wonder if the robot can better understand their computer's needs. As Parisi succinctly put it, "Who knows computers better than a computer?"

Human staff is still available from 7 A.M. to 12 A.M. CST. NaturallyMac can be reached at http://www.ondecktech.com.

The Fiddling Innkeeper

Mark Beaubien arrived in Chicago in 1829 before it was even a town. His taverns were light on the amenities, but rich in hospitality. Beaubien offered the essentials on the prairie: a warm fire, a plate of food, and a mug of whiskey. At the end of the meal, he added his own touch, a tune on the fiddle—anticipating Chicago's passion for good food and lyrical nightlife.

Get Off My Land

On July 10, 1886, Captain "Cap" George Wellington Streeter and crew—his first wife, an engineer, and several passengers—were sailing on Lake Michigan when they crashed into a sandbar along the Chicago lakefront. The land was undeveloped at that time. Streeter looked around, decided he liked the place, and figured that he and his wife and friends could live in the ship so they wouldn't have to pay rent.

Streeter formally dubbed his property "the District of Lake Michigan," whose central governance lay in the ruined hull of his ship, the *Reutan*, which he fortified with an odd assortment of lumber and driftwood. He made some money, charging building developers a fee to dump their debris on the beach near his boat. He claimed he had the authority to extract such fees because the land "'twas a separate commonwealth, under the direct jurisdiction of the United States government." When the region between the *Reutan* and the city shoreline filled with debris, Streeter started renting the landfill to people who built shacks there.

When rich landowners near "Streeterville" complained that the shanties stunk and were lowering their property value, the city stepped in. In July 1889, five cops tried to evict Streeter and his wife, Maria, who drove the trespassing officers off their land with rifles. The city tried to litigate the issue in court for the next ten years. Then in 1899, police apprehended Cap Streeter, but Maria hurled boiling water at the cops, and Streeter drove them off again with his rifle. The following year, a force of 500 officers charged the *Reutan* barricade, but Streeter had organized his own army of hobos and drifters and people who lived on his landfill. The police captured Streeter and his militia, but they were all acquitted in court.

Perhaps it was delusional of Streeter to think that the land was his because he landed on it, much like the first European explorers who set foot on the New World and thought it belonged to them and not to the natives who lived there.

As it turned out, the region where Streeter's ship had run aground belonged to Kellogg Fairbank, a local millionaire. At first, Fairbank had decided to let the captain stay for a while, but when Streeter started selling the landfill, which technically also belonged to Fairbank, the millionaire sued him for forced entry. Meanwhile, in the mid-1890s, other wealthy landowners decided to build a road on the landfill. Streeter tried to stop them. He produced a document, supposedly signed by President Grover Cleveland, saying that he owned the land. But the president's signature was forged. Streeter didn't legally own any of the land, but he kept selling plots to people.

Finally Streeter was apprehended and sent to prison for selling booze illegally on Sunday. His sentence was short, and when he got out of prison, he moved to Indiana with his third wife, Elma Lockwood. Streeter died on January 24, 1921 and is buried in Chicago's Graceland Cemetery.

> Streeter didn't legally own any of the land, but he kept selling plots to people.

Today the region Streeter once occupied extends south from Oak Street to the Chicago River and from Pine Street to Lake Michigan. It includes Navy Pier, the Drake Hotel, the Hancock buildings, and Water Tower Place as well as Northwestern University's Law School, Medical Center, and Business School. Ironically, the neighborhood is known as "Streeterville."

The Perpetual Candidate

Lar "America First" Daly entertained generations of Chicago voters by campaigning for office in an Uncle Sam costume, complete with star-spangled top hat, red, white, and blue tail coat, striped pants, and a faux white goatee. Daly, who had the advantage of a recognizable, but not quite famous name in Chicago (members of the true Daley dynasty have an "e" in their name), was a perpetual candidate throughout the 1950s, 1960s, and 1970s. He ran for more than 40 offices. From president of the United States to school superintendent, U.S. senator and mayor of Chicago, Daly ran a zany, but tireless series of campaigns that left most Chicagoans scratching their heads. He always managed to get a few people to vote for him.

> Daly entertained generations of Chicago voters by campaigning for office in an Uncle Sam costume.

Home Under the Bridge

Richard Dorsay was technically homeless, but immensely inventive. In December 2004, Chicago police discovered Dorsay living in a wooden compartment—complete with television, microwave oven, and assorted video games—tucked inside the Lake Shore Drive Bridge over the Chicago River. Dorsay described how he had transported electric power into his house some time ago, by running extension cords from his "flat" into a power source in the bridge tender's facility. Since the bridge is regularly raised and lowered for river traffic, cops were more mystified at how Dorsay managed to live in a place that was frequently tilting. He explained that whenever the bridge opened, causing his home to tilt, he moved along with the bridge – going from a sitting position to a standing position as the span rose. He admitted it was sometimes scary, but in the end, it was much like living on a Ferris wheel.

The Wimp

Chicago's Southside knew Willie Stokes by his nickname, "The Wimp." To the Chicago Police Narcotics Unit, he was the son of a reputed drug dealer. To the Cook County Coroner, he was a larger-than-life victim of a gang-related murder, one of many in 1984. But most Chicagoans remember his extraordinary funeral worthy of an Egyptian pharaoh. His customized coffin resembled a Cadillac Eldorado, complete with chrome grill and hood ornament. And the embalmed "Wimp" was not lying down, but sitting up behind the wheel of the car with "Bling-bling" diamond rings glistening on every knuckle and crisp $1,000 bills between his fingers.

White Wash

In September 2004, city building inspector Michael Moran was jailed on charges of impersonating a Chicago Police Officer to receive free car washes. Moran allegedly flashed a fake badge to the manager of the Speedy Car Wash at 5724 N. Lincoln Avenue. The manager called police, who pulled up and arrested Moran during the soap-and-rinse cycle. Moran was charged with four counts of theft and four counts of impersonating an officer of the law. On a previous visit to the facility, Moran had signed a log book in which cops record their name and badge number to receive a free wash. Moran was held on $10,000 bail, a high price for auto maintenance.

Yardstick of Presidencies

When Mary Yardley of West Monroe Street died on July 26, 1900, she had lived under every U.S. president from George Washington to William McKinley. She died at 105. If she had only lived another year, she would have seen Teddy Roosevelt inaugurated as well.

My Kingdom for a Nail

Some odd superstitions surround the performing arts. In the theater, for instance, it's considered bad luck to wish good luck. Better to say, "Break a leg" or "Fall off the stage" for the sake of the show. The operatic tenor Luciano Pavarotti refuses to appear on stage without a bent nail in his pocket. He claims that long ago, he found a bent nail backstage moments before the curtain rose, and after the same thing happened a dozen times or so, he regarded a bent nail as a good luck charm and refused to perform without one.

> *The operatatic tenor Luciano Pavarotti refuses to appear on stage without a bent nail in his pocket.*

This curiosity became a crisis in Chicago shortly before an appearance at the Lyric Opera. Before making his entrance in *Tosca*, Pavarotti looked backstage for a bent nail. But the Lyric was so well maintained he couldn't find one. The tenor put his foot down. No bent nail, no performance. Now Pavarotti suspects that, before he performs, the stagehands plant plenty of bent nails backstage where he can easily find them.

Snow Shoveling Fraud

In 1979, Salvatore Mucerino was convicted for snow removal fraud. Forging city employees' signatures on payment forms, Mucerino billed the City of Chicago for snow removal services that he never performed. He received a four-year prison sentence and a $220,000 fine. Despite his conviction, the city later hired Mucerino's firm for $118,000 worth of snow removal.

The Cussing Judge

In December 2004, Cook County Circuit Court Judge Stanley J. Sachs raged against a Chicago cop, who had been found guilty of reckless homicide behind the wheel of his car. Though many empathized with his anger, Sachs raised more than a few eyebrows by uttering the "F" word twice on the bench. The judge was sent off to anger management counseling. Attorneys are now examining whether there are grounds to remove him from sentencing in the case.

Taxi Driver

Paul Barrett, former chairman of the Illinois Institute of Technology's Humanities department, was one of IIT's most popular professors. The historian had an irascible capacity to bring Chicago's earthy character into the classroom and make the city's past flare into life. Barrett had another job as well. He drove a taxicab on weekends to keep in touch, he said, with the vibes of the street.

Quarters

John "Quarters" Boyle got his nickname the hard way. While working for the Illinois State Toll Highway Authority in 1988 and 1989, Boyle pilfered a few quarters at a time—many, many times. He allegedly looted more than $4 million dollars in quarters before getting caught. (If he worked for a full two years, this would mean he stole an average of 30,651 quarters per workday.) Boyle obviously didn't carry all these coins by himself. He had trucks helping him.

Woo-Woo

Ronnie "Woo-Woo" Wickers attends every Cubs game in Wrigley Park. He makes lots of away games as well, since other Cubs fans offer him rides and even buy him airline tickets. Wickers gets all these free rides due to a special talent. He has the loudest cheer. It sounds like a train whistle. His ear-piercing siren call, "WOO-WOO," shatters the roar of the crowd and jars the fillings in your teeth.

If you want to hear what this is like, just flip on a TV or radio broadcast of a Cubs game. Chances are, you'll hear Ronnie in the background.

Meat Mogul's Disassembly Line Inspires Henry Ford

Civil War-era entrepreneur Philip Danforth Armour pioneered the use of refrigeration in the meatpacking industry. Always the opportunist, Armour took advantage of wartime meat shortages to ship "dressed beef" across the country via refrigerated railcars. This meant that meat from the Chicago Stockyards found its way to dining tables nationwide—without spoiling on the way—and Armour & Company put a lot of local butchers out of business. The company's meat-bearing icebox trains sported the slogan "We Feed the World."

Armour's factory innovations also inspired Henry Ford's assembly line. While other plants assigned one butcher to each hog, Armour arranged his workers in a "disassembly line" where each laborer stood in one place and executed one task. A line carried the dead pigs, hanging by their legs, from one worker to the next, until barely a skeleton remained.

> The company's meat-bearing icebox trains sported the slogan "We Feed the World."

Armour & Company sold every part of the pig. The plant produced buttons, drugs, fertilizer, glue, hairbrushes, oleomargarine, and oil, made from animal by-products. But while Armour's factories produced less waste, the sausages sometimes contained sawdust, dead rodents, or rat feces which damaged Armour &

Company's reputation. (Fortunately, federal inspection standards have improved since the nineteenth century.)

In addition to meatpacking, Armour is known for his religious counsel. He suggested that preachers could improve their sermons, "if they included more of Armour's sausages in their diet." He also attributed his success to "keeping [his] mouth shut."

Rodeo in the City Council Chambers

Big Bill Thompson, who served as Chicago's mayor for most of Prohibition, was sharply criticized for his underworld connections. Al Capone was one of Thompson's most generous campaign funders, and Thompson in turn provided the mob leader with police protection.

Thompson engaged in some loony antics. He threatened to punch England's King George V in the nose and to have the public hangman burn all the books in the Chicago Public Library that perpetuated falsehoods concerning Britain's enslavement of other nations, particularly Ireland. His outright anglophobia won the heart of Chicago's large Irish population, and he sailed through three terms largely due to their overwhelming support—though Al Capone certainly helped as well.

Big Bill was an entertaining mayor. He staged a rodeo, complete with horses, in the chambers of the Chicago City Council, like an American version of the

Roman emperor Caligula, who brought his horse onto the Senate floor. The mayor also operated a floating speakeasy, "The Fish Fan Club," masquerading as a yacht in Chicago's Belmont Harbor. Following his 1927 election victory, so many celebrants crowded aboard this boat that the vessel sank, filling the water with so much gin that the harbor was dubbed the world's largest martini.

Council Clash

In 1970, liberal reform candidate Dick Simpson ran for alderman of Chicago's 42nd Ward, a constituency with enough lakefront liberals to provide a strong voter base for someone preaching change, especially from the old time politics of Chicago Mayor Richard J. Daley. Once elected, Simpson wasted no time in challenging the venerable Daley at every opportunity. Simpson, it is far to say, made Daley's blood boil. At one City Council meeting, Simpson, today a professor of Political Science at the University of Illinois Chicago, so angered Daley that the mayor refused to acknowledge Simpson when he stood to be recognized. Simpson refused to back down, and through the entire six-hour Council meeting, Daley kept Simpson standing, refusing to recognize him, and thus prevented him from speaking.

The Astronomer Who Outwitted the Streetcar Magnate

Charles Yerkes pioneered the development of Chicago's "Elevated Electrified," better known as the "El." The "El" went into operation in 1891—beginning the Loop that would eventually circle Chicago's downtown area. This municipal train system revolutionized Chicago's urban space, allowing people to live far from their workplace and commute to work for only a nickel.

But Yerkes was also a ruthless scoundrel. He made and lost his first fortune in Philadelphia, where he served prison time for misappropriating the city's funds. In 1881, Yerkes arrived in Chicago, and in 1886, he launched his mass-transit empire.

In Chicago, Yerkes displayed fewer scruples than in Philadelphia. He opposed legislation benefiting commuters. A "frenzied financier," he issued stocks and bonds exceeding his properties' value. He also bribed the city council to obtain franchises, and when bribery failed, he hired women to seduce and then blackmail the lawmakers.

Yerkes had the worst reputation in town by 1892, the year the University of Chicago opened. In October 1892, university president, William Rainey Harper, and astronomer George Ellery Hale gave the robber baron a chance to redeem his reputation by financing the "world's largest telescope." Harper and Hale neglected to mention that Yerkes would also be expected to build an observatory to contain the instrument, but they did mention it to the press. On October 12, Chicago newspapers announced Hale's inflated account of Yerkes' patronage. Trapped, the magnate reluctantly funded the observatory.

The Yerkes Observatory rose on the shore of Lake Geneva in southern Wisconsin, beyond the reach of Chicago's smog. At the dedication ceremony on October 21, 1897, Yerkes extolled the non-commercial character of astronomy.

From the balcony, Yerkes could glimpse the summer homes of the Chicago social elite who had snubbed him. And they continued to ostracize him, despite his contribution to science. He was, for all practical purposes, run out of town. He resettled in London, where he helped develop another famous subway, the Underground. In *Trilogy of Desire*, novelist Theodore Dreiser modeled his fictional protagonist Frank Cowperwood on the ruthless Yerkes. The trilogy includes *The Financier* (1912), *The Titan* (1914), and *The Stoic* (published posthumously in 1947).

Alphabet Streets

Frank J. Lewis, one of Chicago's most generous philanthropists, endowed universities, hospitals, and other charitable institutions. When he died in 1960, he also left a whole neighborhood filled with "alphabet streets." After World War I, Lewis laid out the grid for a new community on the city's far southeast side, bordering the Indiana State line. He gave the neighborhood everything it needed —sidewalks, streets, alleys, and sewers—except houses. Difficulties in the housing market kept Lewis from constructing homes until after World War II, but the 10th Ward eventually became a thriving community. And Lewis' legacy included 15 streets named after the letters of the alphabet, Avenue A through Avenue O.

A Tangled Web

Walter Kowalski, the longest serving judge in Cook County history, sat on the bench from 1954 until his death in 2001. During this time, he had a long relationship with a Cook County Circuit Court employee, Geraldine Fudema—at least according to Peter Segal, the attorney representing Kowalski's children. Fudema died in 2004, leaving an estate valued between $600,000 and $800,000. She bequeathed $100,000 each to the deceased judge and his sister, Arlene. When Kowalski's widow discovered a financial document bearing the names of her husband and Fudema, she assumed he had left Fudema's funds to her and went to Chicago lawyer Eugene Pilawski, her late husband's attorney, to retrieve the money. Pilawski denied any knowledge of a relationship between his former client and Fudema, but it emerged that Pilawski was Fudema's executor, as well as the recipient of Fudema's pension and Individual Retirement Account. Kowalski's widow and children are now suing Pilawski for embezzling the funds that Kowalski's girlfriend left to Kowalski, who subsequently left the money to his children.

The Devil Came to Chicago

In preparation for the World's Columbian Exposition of 1893, Herman Webster Mudgett, also known as Dr. Henry H. Holmes, constructed his World's Fair Hotel on Chicago's south side at 63rd and Wallace Streets, not far from the fairgrounds. In addition to regular hotel rooms, the edifice included rooms with no windows and airtight doors, an iron-walled gas chamber, and an enormous basement with a kiln that could be heated to 3,000 degrees Fahrenheit. As 27.5 million fairgoers traveled to Chicago for the fair, the handsome, charismatic and psychopathic Holmes welcomed boarders into his hotel. Guests went missing, but the Chicago police didn't investigate. They were too overwhelmed by the millions of people coming to the fair.

No one knows how many people Holmes murdered—at least nine and probably many more. He disposed of his victims' remains in vats of acid and ovens. And he left Chicago before anyone discovered his crimes. A Philadelphia detective, Frank Geyer, finally traced his trail of murders in 1895. Chicago was horribly humiliated. Its police department had no knowledge of the killings. Even more embarrassing, the chief of police had served as Holmes' attorney in a dozen routine lawsuits.

> Holmes welcomed boarders into his hotel. Guests went missing, but the Chicago police didn't investigate.

Holmes was hanged in Philadelphia on May 7, 1896. The undertaker carried out Holmes' instructions for his burial. His body was placed inside a cement-filled coffin then covered with another layer of cement. The coffin was submerged in a cement-filled grave. More cement was poured on top, before the grave was closed.

A number of bizarre things happened after Holmes' death. Detective Geyer fell ill and the warden at the prison where Holmes had been incarcerated killed himself. The foreman of the jury also died in a freak accident and a fire swept through the office of the prosecuting attorney, destroying everything except for a photo of Holmes.

Cubs Criminal

In 2003, the Chicago Cubs had a chance to capture Major League Baseball's National League Championship. In the eighth inning of the key game against the Florida Marlins, Cubs left fielder Moises Alou was diving to snag the ball, when Steve Bartman, a Cubs fan sitting in the front row along the left field foul line, reached out his baseball mitt and interfered with what would have been an easy out. With that snafu, the Cubs' chances of winning evaporated. Wrigley Field security quickly escorted Bartman out of the stadium before the crowd of nearly 50,000 Cubs fans could maul him. Before the start of the Cubs' 2004 season, the infamous ball was destroyed on local television to shake the curse on the Cubs.

Frank Lloyd Wright

Frank Lloyd Wright began his architectural career in Chicago in 1887 with the city's most renowned architect Louis Sullivan and his partner, Dankmar Adler. Wright was 22, but he told everyone he was 20 and continued to fib about his age until his death in 1958. He was Sullivan's protégé, and when he took over a drawing Sullivan had been working on, no one could tell where Sullivan had stopped and Wright had begun.

Sullivan had only one rule—no commissions outside the firm. Wright broke this rule by designing a series of homes in Chicago and suburban Oak Park outside the auspices of Sullivan and Adler. Wright claimed he resigned. Sullivan said he was fired.

> He hired a deranged chef, who murdered his beloved Mamah, her two children, and some of his students.

Continuing to pursue his architectural career, Wright resided in Oak Park, but in 1911, he abandoned his wife and six children and ran off to Europe with the wife of a client, Mamah Bothwick Cheney, who in turn left her family for Wright. Wright called the escapade a "spiritual hegira." Returning from Europe, he feared the ruin of his professional career, so he relocated to Spring Green, Wisconsin, and then to Taliesin. There, he hired a deranged chef, who murdered his beloved Mamah, her two children, and some of his students. Wright survived this tragedy, along with a panoply of financial hardships, bad relationships, and career turns. He gave Chicago the Prairie homes of the early 1900s and the USONIAN designs of the mid-20th century.

Bushman

From the West African nation of Cameroon, Bushman came to Chicago as an infant in 1930. He didn't exactly make his fortune in Chicago, but he was certainly one of the city's most likeable residents—unpredictable, larger-than-life and popular with the females as well. He made Lincoln Park Zoo a center for gorilla breeding. Bushman lived out his years in the Ape House at Lincoln Park Zoo. It's fair to say he was the most famous real ape in the world, rivaled only by the film character King Kong. He drew as many crowds as a Major League Baseball game. More than 120,000 people came to see him in June 1950 alone. He died on January 1, 1951.

Hot Stove

Political hack "Hot Stove" Jimmy Quinn earned his nickname through a phrase he threw around constantly. "That guy would steal a hot stove," he would say, about anyone and everyone. The accusation eventually bounced back on him, and people started calling him "Hot Stove." Given Chicago politics, it's no wonder Jimmy had suspicions.

Newspaper Publisher Breeds Anglophobia

Colonel Robert McCormick, the longtime, larger-than-life publisher of the *Chicago Tribune*, was an ardent Anglophobe. "The Colonel," who had served in World War I military, did his damnedest to sow a deep distrust of the British in the United States. In the late 1880s, McCormick's father was Ambassador Robert Todd Lincoln's second-in-command at the American Embassy in London. Meanwhile, the young McCormick attended the English public school Langley, where the Dickensian treatment of students imbued him with a lifelong hatred of all things British. He also felt that British diplomats had failed to accord his own father proper respect during their time in London.

In the late 1930s, the Colonel tried to use the *Tribune* to turn the American people against President Franklin Roosevelt's plan to aid Britain by lending them tanks and equipment during the war. FDR had to enlist the help of Winston Churchill, McCormick's boyhood friend, to get the publisher to ease up on the anti-British rhetoric.

McCormick, whose grandfather Joseph Medill founded the *Tribune*, is also remembered for coining term "Chicagoland" and holding a contest to select a new headquarters for the paper, the Tribune Tower.

Tree Treasures

Louis Martinez is a thriving Chicago attorney with less time to waste than money, and he has no time to dismantle his holiday decorations. Each year, at the end of the holiday season, he drags his tree, fully decorated with lights, ornaments, and garlands out to his garbage cans. In true Chicago style, his neighbors rip into the tree and take the treasures home.

The Attorney Who Picks Up Trash

Oscar D'Angelo is the "Mayor of Little Italy," an honorary, not an elected post. A practicing attorney, he is known for his service to Chicago's Westside Italian community, and this is not limited to legal services. No one is surprised to see Oscar and his aides stop while driving through the community to pick up garbage or refuse littering the streets and sidewalks. In the roomy trunk of his Cadillac, Oscar carries all the necessary equipment to manicure the neighborhood. His sense of responsibility is as large as his heart.

> In the roomy trunk of his Cadillac, Oscar carries all the necessary equipment to manicure the neighborhood

Plates of Gold

Edith Rockefeller McCormick was the daughter of John D. Rockefeller and one of Chicago's wealthiest heiresses. Her husband, playboy Harold D. McCormick, was the grandson of Cyrus McCormick who invented the reaper, which led to the invention of the International Harvester. But Edith was eccentric. She banned liquor from her home (in a time when this was just not done) and served dinner guests off dishes of pure gold. Edith lost much of her fortune in the Crash of 1929 and spent her remaining years working with Swiss psychologist Carl Jung.

Public Bathrobe

Vito Sessa, longtime employee of the City of Chicago, displayed the old-world Italian roots of his Tri-Taylor Chicago pedigree. The sidewalks and streets of his neighborhood were merely an extension of his family home. He patrolled the neighborhood with ease and comfort, clad in his favorite bathrobe. He was often outside on his block talking to neighbors, giving his opinion or advice—always clad in his bathrobe. He had a curious savvy comfort about him, like Hugh Hefner in his smoking jacket. Local residents would shout, "Hey Vito, how's it going?" And he would respond, "Hey, any day you don't have to work is a great day."

The Window Envelope Fortune

In the late 1890s, Americus Callahan revolutionized business efficiency inventing the window envelope. He donated a generous portion of his window envelope fortune to the University of Chicago. When the school built the Regenstein Library in the late 1960s, they acknowledged Callahan's contribution by designing all the windows in the library in the shape of his window envelope.

Mr. Chicago's Uniform

An award-winning author and darling of left-wing socialist causes, Studs Terkel, also known as "Mr. Chicago," is now in his 90s. In his book *Working*, he interviews a wide swath of Chicagoans to create a social portrait of the city's character. Studs grew up in Chicago. He was the longtime friend of literary giants Nelson Algren and Saul Bellow as well as an early star of Chicago television and an important voice on Chicago radio. But beyond his social and cultural achievements, Studs has a distinctive, all-purpose style of dress. For many decades, he has worn the same clothes every day. His uniform includes a utilitarian navy blue blazer, red gingham shirt, red sweater, gray trousers, and comfortable Hush Puppies suede shoes. Many Chicagoans suspect that he doesn't wear exactly the same threads all the time, but has a closet full of the same clothes.

Indelibly Marked Thieves

Billy Forrester was the most recognizable felon in the city. His body, inked from head to toe, was a living canvass of tattoos.

Popcorn Cochran was a dexterous pickpocket, but he had one liability that marred his career. He was easily identifiable—because he had only one eye. He lost the other one in the early 1880s when "Pinky" Monaghan's peanut roaster blew up on Randolph Street.

Puppy Love

Dora McDonald Barclay was married to Sam Barclay, a turn-of-the-nineteenth-century pitcher for the famed Anson's Colts. But when Sam's arm gave out and he started cutting hair in Chicago, Dora took off. She took up with many men, but finally fixated on the 14-year-old Webster Guerin. Their romance was the talk of the town, until her teenage boyfriend expressed a preference for her niece in 1907. Dora shot Guerin in a rage. She was charged with murder, but her smart lawyer Frank Cain got her a not-guilty verdict that shocked all Chicago. She left town and moved to California.

Self-Fulfilling Prophecy

Charles Stiles was a 32-year old trader when he met 21-year old Madeleine, a beautiful Italian immigrant, at the track in Saratoga Springs, New York, in 1876.

In 1878, Madeleine came to live with him in Chicago. She opened a bordello that brought in lots of cash, but Stiles was plagued by dreams that Madeleine was going to kill him. Their marriage suffered, and one day Charles beat Madeleine, and his dreams came true. She shot him at close range.

Most Marriages

In 1888, Amos Snell, a wealthy Chicago banker was killed mysteriously in the family mansion on Washington Boulevard. His black-sheep son, Albert, raced through his inheritance, leaving little for Amos' daughter Grace. Grace consequently sought out rich suitors—and lots of them. By 1910, she had married 18 times, setting the record for the highest number of marriages for any woman in the United States.

Police Priest

In the 1880s, Captain Peter Kelly of the Chicago Police Department was the only U.S. police officer educated for the priesthood. Kelly had gone to the Irish seminary of St. Patrick's in Maynooth, in County Kildare, but he ran away before being ordained. Arriving in Chicago, he

> Captain Peter Kelly of the Chicago Police Department was the only US police officer educated for the priesthood.

joined the Pinkerton detectives and soon had a career in the Chicago Police Department. Kelly's classical education in Greek and Latin was almost unheard of among his colleagues, and he was the only cop to share an alma mater with the Archbishop of Chicago.

Finding God

"Dead Eye" Dick Lane, a smalltime Chicago safecracker was arrested so often that a local judge threw him out of town in 1897. The despondent Dead Eye was waiting for a train at the Pacific Garden Mission, an evangelical hostel for hobos, drunks, and down-and-outs that proselytized to local thieves and other criminals as well. Most of the hostel's guests didn't heed the call to salvation, but Dead Eye had a mystical conversion experience. He turned from his life of crime and spent the rest of his days preaching at the mission, having found God.

Chicago Pirates

Dick Dooley was a swashbuckling Chicago pirate, fierce and bloodthirsty as any that roamed the seven seas. During the 1870s, he sailed the city's lakefront and riverfront plundering and pillaging with a gusto that Blackbeard would have envied. Before the days of the marine police patrols, Dooley and his partner, "One Night Stand" Cullen, reigned over the city's waterways, raiding warehouses and distilleries and hunting for cargo.

A Gambler of Virtue

Pat Sheedy was a rare man in the underworld of late nineteenth-century Chicago. He was a high-stakes gambler, but aside from that, he was suspected of being a man without vice. He never cursed, smoked tobacco, drank liquor, or consorted with ladies of the night. Despite his flare for big games and high rolling, Sheedy was oddly true to his wife.

Death in Formal Wear

Everyone knew Henry Spencer was a lady killer, but no one took it literally, until Chicago dance instructor Milred Rexroat was found dead with a bullet in her head. She was apparently pregnant with his child and had taken a train out of town with Spencer to get married—or so she thought. Once convicted of murder, Spencer confessed to a series of similar slayings. The hangman at Cook County jail granted his last request—to go to the gallows in a white suit with a red carnation in his buttonhole. Spencer went to his death formally attired.

she was apparently pregnant with his child and had taken a train out of town with Spencer to get married

Cultured Crook

James Harrigan was well versed in classical languages and had a passion for philosophy. He and his elegant French wife hosted salons filled with music and lively conversations on the arts. Despite his scholarly refinement, "Jimmy the Dude" Harrigan was the boss of a rough gang of villains. But before he went out in a blaze of gunfire, he proved that not all mobsters lacked culture.

Sneaky Saint

At the turn of the 20th century, Mother Francis Xavier Cabrini made Chicago a base for her work helping poor Italian immigrants. She established settlement houses, schools, institutes, and hospitals that helped stem the high rate of infant mortality. Her demonstrative personality was an asset to her work. In Chicago, she frequently butted heads with the local hierarchy from whom she demanded assistance. When she caught a cab to see the Archbishop of Chicago in his Chancery Office, she always told her taxi driver to wait for her. Following her meeting, she exited through a rear door, leaving the archbishop to settle accounts with the anxious driver. Apparently, this did not bar her from sainthood. She was the first U.S. citizen declared a saint by the Roman Catholic Church.

Larger than Life

"Oleo" McCarthy, one of the largest individuals on Chicago's Southside, weighed in at more than 500 pounds. During his lifetime, he never trimmed down. When he died in the early 1960s, the undertaker needed piano movers to get Oleo out of his house.

Godfrey's Tavern

Bridie Godfrey owned a saloon on South Halsted Street near Garfield Boulevard. Godfrey's was a well-known establishment, ripe with Irish hospitality and a no-nonsense policy. She was not a woman to be crossed. As a captain's word is law on board a ship, Bridie's was law inside her tavern. Bridie had a beloved Irish setter, who hung out at the bar and lived upstairs with Bridie. One summer day, as the story goes, the dog was running down the hall so fast he couldn't stop. He flew out a large open window without screens and landed in the middle of busy Halsted Street. The bereaved Bridie honored her pet with an Irish wake serving drinks on the house. The line of mourners stretched far down Halsted Street.

Thief Becomes Gardener

Jerry Scalise grew up in Little Italy on Chicago's Westside and graduated from St. Ignatius College Prep, the elite secondary school. Jerry was generally bright, academically gifted and well liked. His biggest critics were the F. B. I. and the Chicago Police, who thought Jerry was up to no good. Frequent run-ins with the law confirmed this.

In the 1980s, Jerry acquired other critics—the Scotland Yard. They claimed he broke into the Burlington Arcade in London and stole the Marlborough Diamond, which the Duke of Marlborough gave to his American fiancée, Sunny Vanderbilt. Scotland Yard produced evidence, and Jerry and his partner, Arthur "the Brain" Rachel, ended up serving time in the British penal system.

> *His biggest critics were the F. B. I. and the Chicago Police.*

Jerry served eight years. During this time, he became an English gardener, and as he was transferred from one prison to another, he added to their botanical beauty. At one prison on the Isle of Wight, he was allowed to remain past his spring transfer date to see his plants bloom. He left each jail a little better than he found it.

Diamond Lil

"Diamond Lil" Arlington was blond, curvaceous, and encrusted with diamonds. Her bailiwick was the rougher, steamier side of 1890s Chicago, and she played on both sides of the tracks—sleeping with cops as well as robbers. She ultimately fell for Dan Kipley, in spite of his penchant for large-scale crime. Kipley was the jealous type. When he caught one of Lil's former boyfriends visiting her at home, he killed the guy. The devoted Lil sold all her diamonds to pay for Kipley's defense and died penniless, waiting for him to get out of jail.

"Mail Box" Mary

"Mail Box" Mary hung out in the Rush Street bars near Division Street in the city's Gold Coast. The cops knew she was turning tricks, and they nabbed her multiple times, but they could never find enough cash on her person to prove that she'd just seen a john. As it turned out, Mary always brought some self-addressed stamped envelopes on her late-night escapades. After she tricked with a john, she placed the cash in an envelope and dropped it into the nearest mailbox before the cops could catch her.

The Real Mickey Finn

In 1896, Mickey Finn opened a dive called the Lone Star Saloon and Palm Garden Restaurant—featuring a single scrawny palm in a pot. From 1883 to 1913, the west side of State Street from Van Buren to Harrison was called "Whiskey Row," because it was lined with saloons. The Lone Star stood at the southern end, between Harrison and Congress, and it was the roughest bar on Whiskey Row. Mickey ran trade school for pickpockets. The Palm Garden was a den of thieves, where his protégés preyed on everyone who dared enter. Mickey also invented a drink called the "Mickey Finn Special" or "Mickey" that knocked its victim unconscious. Mickey's house girls would offer the drink to male customers. When the men passed out, they dragged their victims into backrooms, took their money, stripped off their clothes, and dumped them in the back alley. The phrase "Slip him a Mickey" is still in use, though the police shut down the Lone Star on December 16, 1903. The Chicago Public Library now stands on the site.

Electricity Baron

Samuel Insull, a robber baron from Chicago's Gilded Age, built a $3 billion empire around electricity, which he claimed was a public utility belonging to everyone. People from all walks of life invested in Insull's power company. But when the market crashed in 1929, he lost everything. He left Chicago and died a pauper in a Paris subway station.

The Witch of Roseland

She was known by no other name than La Strega—the witch. And on the streets of Roseland, an Italian neighborhood on the Southside of Chicago, people recognized and feared her. They sometimes swallowed their terror and asked her to tell their fortune or heal a sick child. They said she had the uncanny ability to give people what they were seeking, and she was rarely wrong in what she said.

She could cast the "evil eye" and take it away. Whether or not her powers were real, she provided her community of immigrants with a sense of hope where the local clergy failed.

A Rum Deal

Walter Newberry made his millions in the fluid world of Chicago real estate in the 1840s and 1850s, when, as he said, he "bought land by the yard and sold it by the foot." While sailing to London via the Caribbean islands, Newberry died at sea. Aboard the vessel, little was known about him, except that he was a wealthy and influential man of business from Chicago. Fearing the consequences of burying him at sea, the captain made provisions to preserve Newberry's body so he could send it back to his family when the ship landed. He ordered his crew to open a barrel of rum and store Mr. Newberry inside. After landing in England, he shipped the makeshift casket back to Chicago – where Newberry was interred in the prestigious Graceland Cemetery. Graceland houses the gravesites of many illustrious Chicagoans, but Walter Newberry is the only one who was pickled in a cask of Jamaican rum.

Funeral Home

No one knew his name, but no one could forget where he lived. He resided in a black stretch Cadillac hearse from the 1960s. The boys who went to Mt. Carmel High School on Chicago's Southside would see him every morning, parked along 67th Street in the early hours when they commuted to school. Long before auto-residences were a common sight on city streets, this man was ahead of the curve, living in the roomy compartment of an American funeral car.

First TV Car Salesman

Long before television became the advertising medium it is today, Jim Moran, the owner of Courtesy Motors in Chicago, came up with the idea of selling cars on TV. It was the early 1950s, and the auto industry, along with the rest of the U.S. economy, was just recovering from World War II. Used cars were in high demand. Jim Moran "the Courtesy Man" bought hundreds of old films from Hollywood studios and sponsored a Friday night television show that ran old war movies. During one "live" 11-minute commercial, Moran would display shiny autos at discount prices. No one had thought of selling cars on TV, and marketing-whiz

> During one "live" 11-minute commercial, Moran would display shiny autos at discount prices.

Moran became so successful that on May 24, 1961, his smiling face appeared on the cover of *Time* magazine.

After a health scare, Moran retired and moved to Florida—only to come out of retirement when the founder of Toyota asked him to help launch the Japanese auto in the U.S. Today Moran is worth more than $5 billion. But to Chicagoans, this strange man with the wavy red hair will always be known as Jim Moran "the Courtesy Man."

PART V:
Only in Chicago

I have struck a city—a real city. And they call it Chicago. The other places do not count.

— Rudyard Kipling

Chicago will give you a chance. The sporting spirit is the spirit of Chicago.

— Lincoln Steffens

In the age of global consumer culture, it's hard for any place to claim uniqueness. But Chicago has an unrivaled ability to sell itself. At least eBay buyers think so. In December 2004, the Windy City became the first and so far the only municipality to put itself up for auction on eBay. The auction, offering slices of unique Chicago life to the highest bidder, raised roughly $243,000 in funds for the arts. One winner paid $7,600 for a chance to dye the Chicago River Kelly green on St. Patrick's Day. Another buyer bid $21,000 for a wedding inside the historic Chicago Cultural Art Center. The city proved to the world that it knows how to market itself—in the most bizarre ways.

As we've said before, Chicago has a bit of an inferiority complex. When it can't be "the only," it has to be the biggest, the first, or the best. It's no coincidence that the Windy City boasts the world's largest commercial edifice, the Merchandise Mart; the world's largest public library, the Harold Washington Library Center; the world's largest free public zoo, Lincoln Park Zoo; the world's largest modern art museum, the Museum of Contemporary Art; the world's largest masonry building, the Monadnock Building; the world's longest street, Western Avenue; the world's busiest airport, O'Hare International; the world's largest Tiffany dome, in the Chicago Cultural Center; the world's largest parochial school system, the Archdiocese of Chicago; the world's busiest futures exchange, the Chicago Board of Trade; the world's highest residence above ground, the John Hancock Center; the world's largest municipal harbor system, the Chicago Park District; and the world's busiest sit-down restaurant, the Berghoff. The Windy City has also hosted the largest number of Democratic and Republican National Conventions: 25.

Chicago likewise has an odd array of "firsts," though not all are sources of pride. The city claims the first Republican National Convention in 1860; the first American automobile race in 1895; the first private eye, Pinkerton; the nation's first Red Scare in 1886; the first skyscraper; the first open heart surgery, by

Daniel Hale Williams in 1893; the first blood bank in 1937; the first splitting of the atom in 1942; the first spray paint factory; the first TV car salesman, "Jim Moran, the Courtesy Man"; the first Twinkie; and the first act of sipping champagne from a slipper, at the Everleigh Club in 1902.

But aside from being the only city for auction, Chicago has a number of other unique claims to fame, including the only river that flows backward, the Chicago River; the only holiday lion-wreathing ceremony; the only park district that monitors its work crews by satellite surveillance; and the only chocolate-flavored air, billowing from the Blommer Chocolate Company in the West Loop. In 2004, Chicago also became the first and only city to sell a US highway to a private company. Alderman Edward M. Burke expressed enthusiasm for selling other public roadways and monuments: "I only wish we had something else to sell, like the Brooklyn Bridge." If the Brooklyn Bridge disappears, we'll know whose door to knock on first.

Chicagoland

A mythic creation of *Chicago Tribune* publisher Colonel Robert McCormick, the term "Chicagoland" refers to the surrounding regions that benefit from the city's engine. These include not only the Chicago suburbs, but also the states of Illinois, Indiana, and Wisconsin and sometimes the region from Ohio to the Rocky Mountains. McCormick carefully excluded the decadent East Coast.

A Royal Introduction

In 1860, Queen Victoria's son, "Bertie," the Prince of Wales, later Edward VII, made a brief stop in Chicago while touring Canada. Mayor "Long John" Wentworth, who stood six-foot-six, had the honor of introducing the prince to the members of the Chicago City Council. When the prince arrived, he was ushered into the Chicago assembly. The mayor rose, nodded to the visitor and said, "Prince, the boys. Boys, the Prince." Long John had little patience with protocols or formalities.

Father of the Skyscraper

William Le Baron Jenney (1832–1907) is considered the founder of the first Chicago School of architecture and the father of the American skyscraper. In 1885, he designed the ten-story Home Insurance Building, one of the first structures that used a metal frame, rather than masonry walls, for support. Jenney's design included such features as the elevator and the "Chicago window," two double-hung windows placed on either side of a fixed glass panel. The structure spurred a dramatic reorganization of urban space, as new towers of commerce quickly rose on the flatland of the prairie. The Home Insurance Building, which stood at the corner of LaSalle and Adams Streets, was demolished in 1931.

Chicago for Sale

In December 2004, Chicago became the first municipality to put itself up for auction on eBay—all for the sake of art, of course. Chicago's Department of Cultural Affairs and its savvy culture czarina, Commissioner Lois Weisberg, auctioned off bits of the city's history and unique local experiences to raise funds for the Chicago Cultural Center and other cultural institutions and grants. Items on eBay included:

• the chance to ride along with city plumbers as they dye the Chicago River Kelly green for St. Patrick's Day

• dinner at a Chicago fire house

• a vintage Playboy bunny suit from the 1960s

• a dinner for 12 prepared by Oprah's chef, Art Smith

• dinner for 10 with Chicago TV journalist Bill Kurtis (the item includes a Kurtis documentary interview with the winner)

- the chance to turn on the 45,000 lights around Buckingham Fountain in Chicago's Grant Park esplanade at the start of the 2005 winter season

- a walk-on part at Goodman Theater

- lunch for four with Oprah's design guru Nate Berkus

- dinner with property developer Donald Trump

- a tour of the very private eco-garden on the roof of Chicago's City Hall.

The auction, known as the Great Chicago Fire Sale, ran from December 2 to 16 and raised roughly $243,000 for the arts. The opportunity to dye the Chicago River Kelly green sold for $7,600. Another bidder won a wedding inside the historic Chicago Cultural Art Center for a mere $21,000.

Green River

Chicago is the home of a strange soda pop known as Green River. But Green River is more than just a beverage in Chicago, which has the third largest Irish population in the U.S. Since 1955, when Mayor Richard J. Daley governed Chicago, the city's Irish have celebrated St. Patrick's Day with a giant parade. A brass band, bagpipers, politicians, union workers, high schools, assorted clergy, and visiting dignitaries from the Old Sod march amid the hundreds of floats—all organized by Local #120 of the Plumbers Union, who sponsors the event. The union organizers add one extraordinary touch: they dye the Chicago River. On the day of the parade, a small motorboat winds its way down the river and unloads an organic orange powder that turns the water a shade of bright green. The river stays green throughout St. Patrick's Day, but by the next day it returns to its regular color.

Trapped Under the Rubble

Chicago's Richard Nickel was a gifted photographer whose eye for architecture had a homegrown, prairie feel. His passion was the work of Louis Sullivan, the architect whose organic flourish and modern design gave the city its unique shape and grandeur. His photos trace the sad realities of urban demolition and decay as well as the great architectural achievements. During the 1960s, Nickel watched the preservationists' uphill battle to save the monuments of Chicago's golden past. He grieved the loss of irreplaceable treasures in the name of progress and urban growth. In 1961, Nickel documented the tragic demolition of Sullivan's famed Garrick Theater in a black-and-white film, reminiscent of war footage.

Over the next decade, he grew bolder and more impassioned, decrying the loss of an irreplaceable heritage. His heart broke over the destruction of Louis Sullivan's Chicago Stock Exchange Building. This was perhaps Sullivan's most remarkable work, a structure without equal in its singular form and function. When Nickel lost the fight to save the Stock Exchange, he set out to document the demolition in painstaking detail. Placing himself at great risk, he trespassed into the dark interior with his camera, so that no detail of its design would perish without record.

> This was perhaps Sullivan's most remarkable work, a structure without equal in its singular form and function.

Nickel was planning to take his final shots of the Stock Exchange on April 13, 1972. Before going to bed the night before, he jotted down a small list of sections of the edifice he intended to shoot on the next day. The next morning, he picked up the equipment he needed for his final shots and set out for the Stock Exchange.

Around 1 P.M., some people spotted him striding around the building, angry at some work crew members who were pulling the structure down. That was the last anyone saw of Nickel, until his broken body was found in the rubble of Sullivan greatest work. His death was ruled an accident, owing to the collapse of a section of the old Trading Room floor. His family buried him in the city's Graceland Cemetery, the final resting place of Louis Sullivan, as well as Daniel Burnham and John Wellborn Root, who also helped make Chicago the architectural envy of the world. Nickel's tombstone bears a strong resemblance to the camera through which he witnessed the loss of an irreplaceable Chicago aesthetic.

Daley Controls the Flow of Reported Votes for Kennedy

Richard J. Daley, first elected Chicago mayor in 1955, supported John F. Kennedy from the start. At the 1956 Democratic National Convention, he pushed hard for Kennedy's name on the ticket as vice president.

When Kennedy was nominated for president in 1960, Daley pulled out every stop in the most well-oiled political machine in the U.S. The mayor had the political skills of a Medici and the street smarts of a guerilla fighter. On election day, his minions went out early, canvassing the precincts and insuring that JFK would win in Cook County, the Democratic stronghold of Daley patronage and power. It paid off in what proved to be a squeaky election between Kennedy and Richard Nixon. Nixon, who knew something about thievery, always claimed the election was stolen from him. Some believe that Daley deliberately held back Cook County results until the final moment and helped Kennedy win the election by controlling the flow of reported votes.

Tribune Jumps the Gun

The grandson of *Chicago Tribune* founder Joseph Medill, Colonel Robert R. McCormick served as the editor-publisher of the newspaper from the 1920s to the mid 1950s. "The Colonel" was known throughout Chicago and the publishing world as an irascible demagogue. He was vehemently against the British when they pleaded for aid as war loomed in Europe, and he was equally opposed to Roosevelt as he implemented the New Deal.

The Colonel was no friend of Harry Truman either. He supported former New York Governor Thomas E. Dewey, who challenged the president in the 1948 election. McCormick was so committed to Truman's defeat that he ran the banner headline "Dewey Defeats Truman" on November 5, 1948 before the final election results came in. It was a grand-scale embarrassment for McCormick and a mythic media moment for Truman. Every other newspaper in the United States carried the photo of Truman holding up the front page of the *Chicago Tribune* and laughing uproariously. The rest of Chicago—a largely Democratic city—savored Truman's victory.

Gondola Breeding

Lincoln Park Zoo—the largest free zoological park in the U.S.—opened in 1868. Today it boasts more than 2,000 animals, a state-of-the-art center for primates, and elaborate facilities for its lions, reptiles, and birds. Back in the 1890s, the zoo bought some nearby lagoons and asked for funds to purchase six gondolas that zoogoers could ride on the waterway. One Chicago alderman, Michael Ryan, took umbrage at the expenditure. On the floor of the Chicago City Council, he denounced the wasteful spending. Why did the zoo have to buy so many gondolas? Ryan enshrined himself in Chicago history with the rhetorical question, "Why not just buy a pair and let nature take its course?"

> One Chicago alderman, Michael Ryan, took umbrage at the expenditure.

The Vienna Kosher Hot Dog

Perhaps no food embodies Chicago's curious identity more than the Vienna Kosher Hot Dog, a pure beef sausage born during the World's Fair of 1893. Two young Austro-Hungarian Jewish immigrants, Samuel Ladany and Emil Reichl, perfected a "wiener" which they named in honor of Vienna, their hometown. More than a century later, their kosher line of meats continues to set the standard for everything from corn beefs to pastramis. But their all-beef hot dog has become Chicago's best-loved delicacy, topped by an array of condiments that makes Chicago the hot dog capital of the U.S.

Shakespearean Drama

The great actress Maude Adams came to Chicago in the summer of 1899 to star in the title role in a production of Shakespeare's *Romeo and Juliet*. During one performance, a stage prop caught fire. The crowd was on the verge of panic until —for some reason—the proprietor of the Powers Theater belted out "The Star Spangled Banner." His oddly timed patriotic fervor brought the crowd around.

The Great Flood

Chicago's best-known disaster is the Great Fire of 1871. Few non-Chicagoans know of the catastrophe that wrecked far more havoc—the Great Flood of 1992. The strangest feature of this flood was that every street in Chicago remained dry. The flood occurred in a region of the city that few citizens have ever visited or heard of—the 60-mile network of freight tunnels underneath the Loop.

The freight tunnels have lurked under the city since 1899, when some developers decided that Chicago needed a subterranean railroad that could transport thousands of carloads of freight each day and thus reduce traffic on the streets of the Loop. The developers began digging in secret. They claimed they were constructing a telephone system, when, in fact, they were hollowing out a system of tubes linking all the Loop office buildings that might be interested in paying for a direct freight service. The finished labyrinth covered every block in the greater Loop and was equipped with an electric railway connected to major railroad stations and ports. The plan was abandoned in 1959 after a series of financial setbacks.

In September 1991, some workmen drove new pilings into the riverbed next to the Kinzie Street drawbridge to protect the bridge from traffic on the Chicago River. But the pilings were installed in the wrong place and punctured the ceiling of a freight tunnel.

On the morning of April 13, 1992, more than 124 million gallons of Chicago River water cascaded into the tunnels. As the water filled the tubes, it rose in the basements of downtown commercial buildings. In some structures, the water filled several stories of basements. The flood brought Chicago to a standstill. Businesses shut down. Hundreds of thousands of workers were forced to evacuate their offices. From City Hall to Marshall Fields and from the Circuit Courts to the Board of Trade, underground caverns exhaled strange fishy vapors of marine river life.

Meanwhile, city engineers stuffed sandbags, stones, mattresses, and countless other objects into the cracked floor of the riverbed in an effort to stem the flood. As the sea level rose, Chicago Fire Department officials started pumping water out, but they couldn't keep up with the flood.

Finally, Mayor Richard M. Daley called on the Kenny Construction Company, a move that proved ingenious. They eventually plugged the fissure, stopping the river's flow into the tunnel system.

By the time the waters cleared, the flood had created more than one billion dollars in damages. Some businesses suffered more than others. Department stores absorbed record losses. The city spent months sorting through a second flood of lawsuits and other legal issues. More than three years later, the city paid out more than $36 million in settlements.

> By the time the waters cleared, the flood had created more than one billion dollars in damage.

Today, the tunnel system is outfitted with bulkhead doors to protect it, like those on a submarine. And the Great Chicago Flood of 1992 has taken its place in the city's pantheon of calamity.

The Real Chicago

There is a pecking order among Chicago residents. The "606" zip code distinguishes the city from the suburbs. The same can be said for telephone area codes. All of Chicago was once in the "312" zone. In recent years, a second code, "773" was introduced for neighborhoods outside the core of the downtown. Many Chicagoans found this hard to swallow. Codes "708" and "847" are reserved strictly for the surrounding suburbs. But nothing separates the "real" born and bred Chicagoans from the wannabees more than the pronunciation of the city's name. Outsiders, suburbanites, aliens, visitors, foreigners, and late arrivals all say "sha-CAH-go," while the true locals say "sha-CAW-go." News anchors at the city's media outlets betray their own non-Chicago origins by letting that "CAH" slip out.

The Voice from the Sewer

Chicago has hosted a record number of 25 presidential conventions since 1860, when the city welcomed the first Republican National Convention, which nominated Abraham Lincoln.

U.S. presidential conventions have sometimes served to rally enthusiasm for the candidates, and some aspiring presidents have benefited from their alliance with their host city's political machine. Chicago's machine played an instrumental role in the nomination of Lincoln in 1860 and in the 1940 Democratic National Convention that nominated President Franklin Delano Roosevelt for an unheard-of third term.

Roosevelt almost undoubtedly wanted a third term in office, but with totalitarian regimes looming in Europe, the patrician president did not want to appear to be vying for dictator of the United States. But the big-time party bosses were convinced that the nation needed Roosevelt, and Chicago's homegrown politico Mayor Edward Kelly found FDR's apparent reluctance hard to take.

At the Chicago convention, a message from the president was read, stating that Roosevelt had no desire to be nominated for a third term. Kelly's plan swung into action. As the delegates fell silent, stunned, a voice boomed "We want Roosevelt" through the public address system. "Alabama Wants Roosevelt," the voice shouted, much to the surprise of the Arizona delegation. "Arizona Wants Roosevelt," the mantra proceeded, repeating the verdict for each state. State chairmen looked around to see who was behind this unplanned stampede for the president. They tried to use their microphones, but to no avail. Suddenly, the doors swung open and a parade of Roosevelt supporters marched through the hall, while the organ belted out the popular song, "Franklin Roosevelt Jones"—transforming the Democratic National Convention into a Roosevelt rally.

All this riotous noise finally "persuaded" Roosevelt to concede to his party's wishes and accept the nomination.

The Roosevelt rally may have seemed spontaneous to some, but it was carefully orchestrated. Tommy Geary, Chicago's Superintendent of Sewers, later boasted to the press that he had rigged a microphone into the stadium's public address system and launched the chant as soon as FDR's message was read. Kelly had set Geary up in the stadium's basement and turned off all the other microphones in the hall. Geary earned his place in U.S. history as "the voice from the sewer." Roosevelt was elected and, within months, faced Pearl Harbor and World War II.

> Geary earned his place in US history as "the voice from the sewer."

The Original Hollywood

Long before movie producers discovered that the southern California sun was more conducive to the growth of the motion picture industry, Chicago was the birthplace of the film business. In 1896, Selig Polyscope produced *The Tramp and the Dog*. Selig operated a production company along Irving Park Road, just west of Western Avenue. Passers-by spotted extras—usually Indians and cowboys—

from the sets of Chicago-made movies, riding their horses along Irving Park Road. American Mutoscope-Biograph and the Essanay Studio likewise made motion pictures in the Windy City. Charlie Chaplin supposedly launched his film career in Chicago.

The Windy City remained the U.S. movie capital until World War I, when California's climate and landscape changed the face of American films.

It is hopeless for the occasional visitor to try to keep up with Chicago—she outgrows his prophecies faster than he can make them. She is always a novelty; for she is never the Chicago you saw when you passed through the last time.

— Mark Twain

Nobel Natives

The University of Chicago boasts 78 Nobel Laureates among its faculty: three in Literature, 11 in Physiology or Medicine, 15 in Chemistry, 26 in Physics, and 23 of the last 50 in Economic Sciences. The renowned Quadrangle Club near campus reserves special tables for Nobel Prize winners. It is nice to know they don't have to wait for a table at lunch.

Spray Paint—A Sin Most Vile

In the 1990s, the Chicago City Council passed a law banning sale of spray paint, in an effort to stamp out tagging, the act of spray painting public buildings with graffiti. Only one high-end art supply store sells spray paint—and only after a security clearance. Some say it's easier to buy a gun in Chicago than a spray paint can.

The city's emergency urban response team handles all spray paint incidents, no matter how seemingly benign. At the tiniest sign of tagging, the mayor's Graffiti-Busters rush to the rescue and blast the graffiti with their power washers, making quick work of the offending art.

> The city's emergency urban response team handles all spray paint incidents, no matter how seemingly benign.

Ironically, spray paint is a Chicago invention. In 1949, Edward H. Seymour patented a technique for spraying paint from an aerosol can. He later established the nation's first spray paint factory in the Windy City.

Death Misses the Archbishop

When George Mundelein was appointed archbishop of Chicago in 1916, the city threw a gala luncheon at the Palmer House Hotel. During the meal, the archbishop passed on a bowl of soup, which most of the other guests enjoyed. Those who did ended up in the hospital. The chef in the hotel's kitchen had laced the soup with arsenic. Many suffered, but the dosage was too mild to kill anyone.

Cartoon Characters

Irish saloonkeeper Martin J. Dooley and Polish worker Slats Grobnick lived almost a century apart. Actually, they never lived at all. As fictitious characters, they were perhaps more free to do and say as they pleased. Dooley, created in the 1890s by Finley Peter Dunne of the *Chicago Journal*, dispensed a cracker barrel type of wisdom while chiding the antics of "Tiddy Roooseyvelt," and local Chicago pols.

Grobnick, whom Mike Royko invented for the *Chicago Tribune* in the 1990s, had a no-nonsense way of cataloguing the goings-on inside City Hall. Royko made piñatas out of the two Mayor Daleys and an assortment of local robber barons. Both Dunne and Royko embody the brand of political journalism that thrives in the Windy City.

Alligator Denial

Elected in 1983, Harold Washington, Chicago's first African-American mayor, possessed an uncommonly elegant, almost Victorian mastery of the English language. The Chicago press was no match for his special brand of candor and perplexing King's English. Once as the mayor was making his way to his City Hall office, a member of the press caught him off-guard. The mayor disconcerted everyone with his response—"I deny the allegation, and I deny the allegator."

Airport Confusion

In Chicago's O'Hare International—the world's busiest airport—travelers are endlessly flummoxed by the three-letter code on their luggage: ORD. LAX (Los Angeles International) and LAG (New York's LaGuardia) cause only minor mayhem compared to the Chicago acronym. Few realize that ORD was in use before the 1950s, when the airport was renamed after World War II flying ace, Lt. Commander Edward J. O'Hare. Before that, O'Hare was a small airport named Orchard Field, hence the letters ORD.

Football Trouncing

The University of Chicago has more of a reputation for splitting atoms than for football. But the school once boasted one of the most successful inter-collegiate football teams in the nation. Amos Alonzo Stagg, the father of inter-collegiate sports and "grand old man of football," organized U of C athletics in the 1890s and coached the football team until 1933. On November 11, 1899, the University of Chicago defeated Northwestern by an unprecedented 76-0. The game remains one of the greatest defeats in college sports.

A founding member of the Big Ten college athletic conference, University of Chicago won seven Big Ten football titles between 1895 and 1939, when it disbanded its football team as part of a trend to de-emphasize varsity athletics. Since 2000, the University of Chicago has even had a "dance squad," the Phoenix Fires, who performs at football games. This sets the Maroons apart from the Chicago Bears, who have no cheerleaders—a strange phenomenon in a nation where football and cheerleaders tend to go hand in hand. The Bears nonetheless have a curiously suggestive slogan, "Bear Down Bears!"

Capone Kaput

Al Capone was Chicago's most notorious gangster—the kingpin of the city's underworld during Prohibition. On January 25, 1947, Capone died in Miami, Florida, following a long bout with syphilis and a fatal stroke. He had been out of town for eight years, serving a prison sentence for tax evasion. Nonetheless, he was buried on the city's Southside in Mount Olivet Cemetery along busy 111th Street, where admirers made pilgrimages to his grave. According to Italian custom, the tombstone displayed an oval photo-ceramic portrait of Capone. But the photo kept disappearing, since visitors could not resist the temptation of a free souvenir. Irked at these acts of vandalism, Capone's family had his body secretly removed from Mount Olivet and re-interred in Mount Carmel, a newer cemetery west of the city. Ironically, the mob boss rests in the same hallowed grounds as Chicago's Roman Catholic Archbishops. Capone's grave also lies near the stones of his archenemy, rival mob boss Dion O'Bannion, and of future crime bosses, Tony "Big Tuna" Accardo and Sam Giancana.

> The mob boss rests in the same hallowed grounds as Chicago's Roman Catholic Archbishops.

Great Fire Survivors

Five public buildings that survived the Great Fire of October 8, 1871 are still standing. These include the Water Tower, St. Ignatius College Prep at 1076 West Roosevelt Road, Holy Family Catholic Church at 1019 S. May Street, St. Patrick's Catholic Church at 718 West Adams Street, and First Baptist Congregational Church at 60 North Ashland Avenue.

It's All Greek

Gyros is a savory Greek dish—a curious blend of beef and lamb, ground and reformed into a large cylinder that cooks rotisserie-style. Heavily scented with garlic and herbs, it has almost become a fast food symbol of Greek cuisine. Oddly enough, gyros was not invented in Greece. It was the brainchild of Chris Tomaras, a Greek immigrant living in Chicago's Greek Town on South Halsted Street in 1975. It became so popular that it spread across America, and eventually to Greece too.

Born in Chicago

Comedian Jack Benny, Tarzan creator Edgar Rice Burroughs, cartoonist and filmmaker Walt Disney, author and TV producer Michael Crichton, playwright David Mamet, comedian Bob Newhart, actress Gloria Swanson, U.S. Senator and former First Lady Hillary Rodham Clinton, musician Benny Goodman, U.S. Secretary of Defense Donald Rumsfeld, Olympic figure skater Dorothy Hamill, actress Kim Novak, writer Ben Hecht, architect Frank Lloyd Wright, writer Ernest Hemingway, the *X-files'* Gillian Anderson, former First Lady Betty Ford, singer Phil Everly, actors Martin Mull, Joe Mantegna, Mandy Patinkin, and Aidan Quinn, actress Rachel Welch, First Lady of California Maria Shriver, the Simpson's Dan Castellaneta, and blues legend Curtis Mayfield were all born in Chicago. Oh yeah, and Mr. T.

Too Hot?

Around 1899, the University of Chicago forbade the student band from playing "A Hot Time in the Old Town Tonight." Were they trying to prevent the Great Fire from being trivialized, or was the tune too risqué for a university with Baptist roots?

Wheeling and Dealing

The Chicago Skyway, a 7.8-mile toll road built in 1958, connects the city to the Indiana Tollway System. In the autumn of 2004, the city leased the aging skyway to a commercial venture called Centra-Maquarie for 99 years for an unbelievable $1.82 billion. The consortium, an Australian/Spanish partnership, is required to pay the $1.82 billion in a lump sum within 90 days of signing the lease. This agreement marks the largest single financial deal in Chicago's history and the first time a U.S. highway has been transferred from public ownership to private.

> This agreement marks the largest single financial deal in Chicago's history.

Expressing his enthusiasm, longtime Chicago Alderman Edward M. Burke raved, "Not since the Dutch bought the Island of Manhattan for 60 Guilders

($24) has there been such an amazing deal." The remark was an unfortunate slip and one that could hardly have comforted Centra-Maquarie. The story of the 1626 Dutch purchase of Manhattan from the Indians for $24 is probably more fiction than fact, but for Native Americans, the tale embodies how the European settlers stole their land. (It's worth noting that when a group of Indians occupied Alcatraz in 1969, they jokingly offered to pay the U.S. government "$24 in glass beads and red cloth" for the island.)

The alderman added another odd comment: "I only wish we had something else to sell, like the Brooklyn Bridge." If the Brooklyn Bridge disappears, at least we'll know whose door to knock on first.

Mob Monikers

In the 1920s through the 1950s, Chicago came to know its mobsters through the endearing names they received in the press. Joseph Lombardo, known for joking around with his buddies, acquired the name "Joey the Clown" Lombardo. Joseph Aiuppa, a former boxer known as Joey O'Brien, was "Joey O'Brien" Aiuppa. Murray Humphreys earned the name Murray "The Camel" Humphreys for his stylishness and preference for camelhair coats. Charles Gioe was dubbed "Cherry Nose" Gioe on account of his large olfactory organ. Paul Ricca, who once worked in a restaurant, was affectionately known as Paul "The Waiter" Ricca. Al Capone was, of course, Scarface.

Police With Style

For a short time in the fall of 2004, it looked as though members of the Chicago Police Department's Targeted Response Unit would be donning a touch of French fashion. The department considered adding berets to the dress code. After some discussion, they decided on a more American accessory—baseball hats instead of berets.

Bus Busting

Cameras recently installed on Chicago Transit Authority buses have nabbed more than 400 drivers who ignore the "bus only" lanes on Chicago streets. Another 2,700 motorists escaped the $90 fine, due to technical difficulty. Once the cameras start working properly, the system will free up traffic lanes and net the city a nice piece of change.

Gang Warfare

During a recent funeral for a slain Latin Kings gang member, cars proceeding to Chicago's Resurrection Cemetery were traveling along Archer Avenue, near 63rd Street, when they passed a rival gang member along the route and opened fire. The wounded individual was allegedly flashing rival gang signs as the funeral passed.

Frankenfish

In October 2004, a fisherman netted an 18-inch fish with grisly fangs in a harbor near downtown Chicago. Scientists with the Illinois Department of Natural Resources identified the fish as the northern snakehead, native to China, Korea, and Russia. This voracious predator, also known as "Frankenfish," can breathe air while wriggling short distances across land and thus skips from one body of water to another. The northern snakehead can reach a weight of 15 pounds and a length of 40 inches. Scientists consider it ecologically menacing. The razor-toothed fish can devour frogs, birds, and mammals, as well as other fish. If the Frankenfish breeds, it could wipe out game fish and thus ruin the Great Lakes' multibillion-dollar fishing industry.

"These things are voracious feeders. They're a very aggressive fish," said Department of Natural Resources' Mike Conlin. Teams used electric cables to shock fish to the surface of the harbor, but so far they haven't found any other northern snakeheads.

Great Lakes authorities have been battling invasive species for some time—most recently the Round Goby, Zebra Mussel and Sea Lamprey. Work crews recently constructed an electrified underwater barrier to prevent Asian Carp from migrating from the Mississippi River watershed into Lake Michigan. When frightened, the Asian Carp can sometimes leap out of the water and knock people out of boats.

Democratic Landslide

In the recent presidential election of 2004, Chicago's Cook County, a longtime Democratic stronghold in the Midwest, recorded the largest margin of victory for Presidential candidate John Kerry anywhere in the United States, with more than 800,000 votes. Los Angeles County was second.

Judge Campaigns for Self in Court

It was unorthodox, to say the least, even by Chicago pre-election stunts. Cook County Criminal Court Judge Bertina E. Lampkin ruffled her colleagues' feathers and stirred media interest in 2004, when she sent out letters asking the jurors who sat in her court to vote for her.

People were appalled. But while Lampkin's shameless self-promotion may have crossed a line of propriety, it did not break any law. Some say there is no such thing as bad publicity. This may be true, seeing that Judge Lampkin was, in fact, re-elected.

Philanthropic Professor

Frank Untermyer was a grandson of Samuel Untermyer, the hard-nosed trust-busting attorney who shattered the monopoly once enjoyed by Standard Oil. From 1946 until 1982, Frank Untermyer was a professor of political science and African studies at Chicago's Roosevelt University. Following his recent death, it was discovered that over the course of his tenure with the university, he had been a secret scholarship sponsor to hundreds of students, especially from African nations. His was a quiet philanthropy.

City Farm

Few people might realize it, but the City of Chicago maintains a 72-acre working farm within city limits. On the far southwestern edge of the city, near 111th Street and Pulaski Avenue, 585 high school students attend the city's agrarian laboratory. There is no school like it anywhere in the Midwest. Recently, students observed the first birth of a calf on the farm in decades. The school offers a wide array of agricultural sciences, and students get hands-on experience looking after the farm's livestock, including three head of cattle, two pigs, chickens, and a racehorse.

> Recently, students observed the first birth of a calf on the farm in decades.

World's Greatest Network

Chicago's WGN radio station once had the nation's strongest radio signal. Reaching far beyond the city limits, it provided a news and entertainment lifeline to the entire Midwest. In the heyday of radio, the station gave the nation radio favorites such as Amos and Andy, Fibber McGee and Molly, Jack Armstrong, and the Breakfast Club.

In March 1929, WGN embarked on an experiment that led to the police radio systems used today. The station started interrupting local radio shows to broadcast emergency bulletins to cops in their squad cars. Of course, everyone who tuned into the station heard about police emergencies—including the local crooks.

> WGN embarked on an experiment that led to the police radio systems used today.

First U.S. Car Race

In 1895, the first automobile race in the United States took place in Chicago. The track stretched from Chicago to Evanston, Illinois. J. Frank Duryea won the race, averaging a breathtaking speed of 7.5 miles per hour.

A Deep and Lasting Influence

In 1943, Chicago restauranteer Ike Sewell introduced a pizza with a thick cornmeal crust, reminiscent of the "rustico"-style Roman peasant pizza. His Uno's and Due's Pizzerias still serve these "Chicago-style pizzas"—also known as "deep dish" pizzas.

During the Depression, a Chicago baker invented a cream-filled sponge cake, which he later sold to the Hostess Baking Company. The Twinkie was born.

Eli Schulman owned Eli's The Place For Steak, frequented by local politicos and Hollywood luminaries. But Eli's cheesecake eclipsed his steaks and became a separate enterprise, Eli's Chicago's Finest Cheesecake, in contrast to "New York-style" cheesecake.

Chocolate Plant Produces Chocolate Air

A Chicago fixture since 1939, Blommer Chocolate Company boasts the largest cocoa bean roasting operation in America and manufactures more cocoa butter and cocoa power than any enterprise in the country. The company's plant at 600 West Kinzie Street also produces chocolate-flavored air, a buttery cocoa scent suffuses the west Loop of the Windy City and mystifies tourists.

Save the Birds

In the late nineteenth century, Burnham and Root, Sullivan and Adler, and William Le Baron Jenney founded what is known as the first Chicago School of architecture. Ludwig Mies van der Rohe founded the second Chicago School. The German-born architect helped define mid-20th-century modernist architecture, by designing edifices that embodied the industrial age. The campus of the Illinois Institute of Technology encompasses 20 of Mies' buildings, including his masterwork, S. R. Crown Hall, completed in 1956. Crown Hall's glass and steel cubes are simple in design, yet confounding to birds, which have been smashing into the massive windows for five decades. But ITT is showing greater concern for environmental issues. As Crown Hall undergoes restoration, work crews are moving the trees inside the building away from the window and installing opaque lighting—in the hope of protecting our feathered friends.

> Crown Hall's glass and steel cubes are simple in design, yet confounding to birds

Municipal Carjacking

In 2003, Adrienne Leonard was traveling overseas, when her mother phoned. The City of Chicago had booted and towed her green 2001 Kia Sephia from the street in front of her home. When Leonard went to retrieve her auto, she discovered that her three parking tickets plus towing and storage fees totaled $1,000, and she only had 15 days to raise the funds. When she failed to pay her fines in time, the city claimed ownership of her vehicle and sold it for $125.54. On top of her parking fines, Leonard still owes $13,800 on the loan for her car. Her plight inspired a full-scale investigation by the *Chicago Sun Times*. The newspaper claims that the city tows 170,000 cars each year, and some 70,000 are never returned. The plot thickens.

Stylish Stickers

If you own a car in Chicago, you must display your vehicle stickers in the lower right-hand corner of your windshield. All city stickers once had that official made-by-a-government-agency look. But no longer.

Each year, adolescent artists from over 40 high schools in Chicago submit more than 500 designs for next year's stickers. After a selection committee chooses 10 finalists, Chicagoans vote by phone or internet on their favorite design.

Walt Disney

One of Chicago's public high schools is named after Walt Disney, the creator of cartoon characters Mickey Mouse and Donald Duck. The Disney family helped fund the school's new animation lab, and Diane Disney Miller showed up for the dedication.

Walt himself grew up in Chicago and attended the city's McKinley High School. His first cartoons appeared in the McKinley High School paper.

Assassination Shutdown

When news of President Abraham Lincoln's assassination reached Chicago, the Land of Lincoln's main city shut down. All shops, saloons, and theaters closed. So did the courts and the Chicago Board of Trade. Sunk in mourning, the city prepared for Lincoln's funeral train, which stopped in Baltimore, Harrisburg, Philadelphia, New York, Albany, Buffalo, Cleveland, Columbus, Indianapolis, and Chicago, before reaching Lincoln's hometown of Springfield, Illinois for burial. When the train arrived in Chicago on May 1, 1865, the entire city turned out to welcome Lincoln back to Illinois.

But a piece of Illinois had been with the funeral train since it left Washington, D.C. A Pullman Sleeper—a railroad coach designed for comfortable overnight travel—was attached to the train bearing Lincoln's body.

This was great advertising for George Pullman and Ben Field, who had just started manufacturing the Sleepers in 1865. When spectators saw the Pullman car attached to Lincoln's funeral train, the demand for sleeping cars skyrocketed.

The Tribune Tower

When *Chicago Tribune* publisher Colonel Robert McCormick wanted a new home for his newspaper, he sponsored an architectural contest. The contest resulted in a dramatic new building, the Tribune Tower. Completed in 1925, it stands at Michigan Avenue and the River.

As if unsatisfied with its own renown, the Tribune Tower's gothic entrance contains stones from other famous buildings, including Westminster Abbey, Cologne Cathedral, the Alamo, the Taj Mahal, the Great Pyramid, and the Arc de Triomphe.

Trolley Trip

Four-wheel trolleys still run along the streets of downtown Chicago, shuttling visitors mostly from one tourist attraction to another. During the holiday season, the city adds a special twist—all trolleys are free. Tourists and local shoppers alike can take advantage of the free network, bustling between train stations, museums, parks, the zoo, and department stores. Trolleys run from 10 A.M. to 8 P.M. and are free from the day after Thanksgiving until the day after New Years. Tired, irritated shoppers relish the ride from one bargain to another. What's so strange about this? Well, anything free in the U.S. is weird.

Margie's Magic

Margie's Candies on Western Avenue is a slice of American life that no longer exists in most cities. Since 1921, Margie's has made two favorites: homemade ice cream and hand-dipped chocolates. Little has changed in the past 80 years. Swank Chicagoans still go to Margie's for dessert after dining in local restaurants. Rumor has it that in the 1920s, Margie's was Al Capone's favorite place for sundaes.

Chicago sounds rough to the maker of verse. One comfort we have— Cincinnati sounds worse.

– Oliver Wendell Holmes

Morrison Hotel

Chicago's Morrison Hotel was a monster of a building, constructed in four successive stages between 1913 and 1932. With 3,400 rooms, it was one of the world's largest hotels. In 1965, the wrecking ball demolished the hotel to make room for the modern headquarters of the First National Bank, now Bank One.

Chicago Imagist

Ed Paschke (1939–2004), a lifelong Chicagoan, was considered one of the Chicago Imagists—a branch of Pop Art that borrowed from Surrealism, outsider art and pop culture. But Paschke alone based his neon-colored figure paintings on photos culled from magazines, newspapers, and TV. A fan of urban subcultures, Paschke drove around with a carload of jackets, and as he visited Chicago nightclubs and bars, he changed clothes according to the neighborhood and the clientele.

> But Paschke alone based his neon-colored figure paintings on photos culled from magazines, newpapers, and TV.

Pet Savior

Under the present municipal code, any animal in the pound for more than 10 days can be "donated" to a hospital, institution of learning, or laboratory. This includes pets with license tags whose owners have not yet claimed them. Gene Schulter, alderman of the city's 47th Ward, became Chicago's latest hero when he introduced a resolution to overturn the current law and keep potential pets safe from science.

Festive Fares

In some cities, festive garland and lights signal the approach of the holidays. But in Chicago, strictly enforced parking bans go hand in hand with yuletide cheer. From Thanksgiving through April, overnight parking is out of the question on the city's main thoroughfares. Anyone who has survived a Chicago snowstorm understands the method to this madness. When the main arterial streets are clear of parked cars, snow removal is a breeze. Careless car owners who fail to note the change of seasons know the bottom line—a $50 parking ticket and a $150 tow.

Wreathing of the Lions

Chicagoans gather each yuletide for an unusual holiday festivity—the wreathing of the lions at the Art Institute of Chicago. A true Chicago treasure, the maned and muscled felines have stood watch at the Michigan Avenue entrance since 1894. The work of acclaimed animalier Edward Kemeys, the sculptures measure ten feet from nose to tail. The beast on the north side raises his tail and bares his teeth, while his companion on the south keeps his tail lowered and maws closed. Each holiday season, the lions are adorned with luxurious balsam wreaths encircling their necks. The wreathing has become a Chicago tradition, replete with carols and holiday pomp.

> *The wreathing has become a Chicago tradition, replete with carols and holiday pomp.*

Lettuce Entertain You

For almost 30 years, Lettuce Entertain You Enterprises (LEYE) has offered Chicagoans an imaginative array of restaurants—from vintage 1950s hamburger joints to French bistros and Italian trattorias. These eateries are as much a part of Chicago as a Cubs game. You can tell a true Chicagoan by the number of LEYE she can rattle off. There are dozens.

LEYE founder Rich Melman often patrols his food empire with fork and knife in hand. He tests the food cooking in his kitchens with old-fashioned quality control—one bite at a time.

Fire Monument

The Great Fire of 1871 razed three-fifths of the central city, but the memorial is modest compared to the damage. Egon Weiner's bronze "Pillar of Fire" stands at Jefferson and DeKoven Streets. The sculpture marks what was long considered ground zero of the inferno—the site where Catherine O'Leary allegedly tipped over a lantern while milking her cow. This site lay on the outskirts of the city in 1871, but today it is the home of Chicago's Fire Academy.

Caryatids

Surrounded by a bold, muscular cityscape, Chicagoans have a refined taste for architecture. Their skyline ranks third after New York and Hong Kong. But if you ask residents their favorite structures, many will name the 24 lovely ladies who serve as support columns along the west side of the Museum of Science and Industry. The Caryatids were part of the original beaux arts exterior of the Palace of Fine Arts, which Charles C. Atwood designed for the 1893 World Columbian Exposition. Later the structure was converted into the Museum of Science and Industry, which opened in 1933. Among many exhibits, visitors can walk through a 20-foot-tall model of the human heart.

The Unsleeping Eye

Most Americans think of the Secret Service as those stiff pokerfaced bodyguards in suits and dark glasses who stand around the chief of state. This agency didn't exist when Abraham Lincoln was elected as president.

> What if some angry southerners attacked his train line as it carried Lincoln to his swearing-in?

In 1861, when Lincoln traveled from Chicago to Washington, D.C. for his inauguration, the federal government took no special precautions. But Samuel Felton, president of the Philadelphia, Wilmington and Baltimore Railroad, couldn't sleep. The nation was bitterly divided. After Lincoln's election, seven states had left the Union and formed the Confederate States Of America. What if some angry southerners attacked his train line as it carried Lincoln to his swearing-in?

The panicked Felton called on Scottish-born Allan Pinkerton, the United State's first private eye, based in Chicago. Pinkerton placed agents all along the route from New York to Washington. The detectives didn't hear of any plans to attack the railroad, but instead they unraveled a plot to kill Lincoln on the way to his inauguration after his train stopped in Baltimore's Calvert Rail Station. Baltimore's chief of police was in on the conspiracy and had deployed minimal police protection, so that the assassins could get to Lincoln quickly and easily.

During the Civil War, Lincoln and General George B. McClellan saw the need for a federal espionage agency and appointed Pinkerton as head of the "Secret Service" under the Department of War. This first Secret Service was short-lived. When the president fired McClellan, he ditched Pinkerton too. Later, in 1865, Lincoln created another Secret Service, a bureau of the U.S. Treasury Department, to crack down on counterfeit money. This Secret Service only took on the task of protecting the president after the assassination of President William McKinley in 1901.

Pinkerton always claimed that if he'd still been working for the feds in 1865, John Wilkes Booth never would have put a bullet in Lincoln's head. But Pinkerton went back to his own private sleuthing in Chicago, and his Pinkerton Detective Agency lives on to this day.

A Lot of Water

Chicago's Shedd Aquarium remains the world's largest aquarium and the only inland aquarium boasting both freshwater and saltwater exhibits. More than 200 tanks display aquatic life from around the planet. The coral reef tank in the original aquarium contains 90,000 gallons of water. A new Oceanarium, which opened in 1990, houses a two million gallon whale tank. Another 120 tanks hold two million gallons of seawater on reserve. The facility now produces its own salt water. But until 1970, Shedd received trainloads of seawater from Key West, Florida, as much as one million gallons at a time.

> *The coral reef tank in the original aquarium contains 90,000 gallons of water.*

John Graves Shedd, president of Marshall Field & Company from 1906 to 1922, died before the Aquarium opened. His elegant mausoleum in the city's Rosehill Cemetery features a Tiffany window portraying a rich array of aquatic life.

Execution Moratorium

On August 24, 1962, James Dukes was the last occupant of Chicago's electric chair in the basement of the Cook County Jail. The state of Illinois has a rather spotted record for sentencing innocent people to death. Since capital punishment was reinstated in 1977, the state has put 12 convicts to death and freed 13 inmates who were wrongly convicted. In January 2000, then Governor George Ryan declared a moratorium on all executions, saying, "There's a flaw in the system, without question, and it needs to be studied." The moratorium is still in effect.

SOURCES

Bielski, Ursula, *Chicago Haunts: Ghostly Lore of the Windy City,* Lake Claremont Press (1998).

Chicago Sun-Times (December, 2004).

Chicago Tribune (February 18, 2005).

Cincinnati Enquirer (1876).

Cincinnati Enquirer (February 12, 1877).

Danckers, Ulrich, "French Chicago During the 18th Century," *Baybury Review* (1997).

Davey, Monica, "Tribute to Chicago Icon and Enigma," *New York Times* (June 25, 2003).

DelBanco, Andrew, "Introduction, *The Portable Abraham Lincoln,*" New York, Penguin (1992).

Drexel, Allen, "Before Paris Burned: Race, Class, and Male Homosexuality on Chicago's South Side, 1935–1960," in Brett Beemyn, ed. *Creating a Place for Ourselves: Lesbian, Gay, and Bisexual Community Histories,* Routledge (1997).

Franch, John, "Charles Tyson Yerkes, 1837–1905," University of Chicago Alumni Magazine (February 1997).

Gugliotta, Guy, "The Robot With the Mind of an Eel: Scientists Start to Fuse Tissue and Technology in Machines," *The Washington Post* (April 17, 2001).

Kaczmarek, Dale, *Windy City Ghosts,* Whitechapel Productions (2000).

Larson, Erik, *The Devil in the White City,* New York: Crown (2003).

Lukas, J. Anthony, *The Barnyard Epithet and Other Obscenities: Notes on the Chicago Conspiracy Trial,* New York: HarperCollins (1970).

Meek, James, "Robot with living brain created in US," *Guardian* (April 18, 2001).

Pittsburgh Post-Gazette (2005).

Rasmussen, Cecilia, "The Painful Ordeal of Tokyo Rose," *Los Angeles Times.*

Taylor, Troy, "Bathhouse John, Hinky Dink and Others: Chicago's History Of Graft and Corruption," *New York Times* (August 28, 2004).

users.vnet.net/schulman/
Columbian/ferris.html#TOP

University of Chicago Alumni Magazine (February 1997).

Wendt, Lloyd and Herman Kogan, *Lords of the Levee: The Story of Bathhouse John and Hinky Dink,* New York: Bobbs-Merrill Co. (1943).

www.billygoattavern.com/
history.html

www.bloodbook.com/
trans-history.html

www.chicagohistory.org/dramas/
act1.html

www.chicagohistory.org/dramas/
overview/over.html

www.chipublib.org/004chicago/
timeline/originame.html

www.corsinet.com/chicago/
chicagot.html

www.crimelibrary.com

www.dmregister.com/news/stories/
c4788998/22247528.html

www.earlychicago.com/
encyclopedia.php?letter=C

www.eprairie.com/releases/
viewrelease.asp?postID=390

www.geocities.com/~jimlowe/sally/
sallydex.html

www.guardian.co.uk/print/

0,3858,4171567-103681,00.html

www.kensmen.com/tokyorosec.html

www.law.umkc.edu/faculty/projects/
ftrials/Chicago7/Account.html

www.law.umkc.edu/faculty/projects/
ftrials/leoploeb/LEO_LOEB.html

www.law.umkc.edu/faculty/projects/
ftrials/leoploeb/LEO_LEOP.html

www.laweekly.com/ink/printme.
php?eid=56457

www.ling.ed.ac.uk/linguist/issues/12/
12-3157.html

www.nytimes.com/2004/12/25/
national/25ymca.html?ex=1112245
200&en=cbc29949b7222d6a&ei=5
070&ex=1104642000&en=257b85a
21800a954&ei=5006&partner=ALT
AVISTA1

www.onphilanthropy.com/
prof_inter/pi2005-01-14.html

www.pbs.org/wgbh/amex/chicago/
peopleevents/p_armour.html

www.prairieghosts.com/graft.html

www.prairieghosts.com/leopold.html

www.princeton.edu/~mcbrown/
display/williams.html

www.readersdigest.co.uk/magazine/
Pavarotti.html

www.showmensleague.org/
showmens_rest/
showmens_rest.html

www.straightdope.com/classics/
a990917.html

www.suntimes.com/special_
sections/almanac/ghosts.html

www.wehaitians.com/tribute%20to%
20chicago%20icon%20and%20
enigma.html

www.yourhometown.org/
page15.html